A Funny Thing Happened

On My Way Through

the Bible

Brad Densmore

BARBOUR
PUBLISHING, INC.
Uhrichsville, Ohio

A Funny Thing Happened

On My Way Through

the Bible

© MCMXCVIII by Brad Densmore.

ISBN 1-57748-215-8

Published by Barbour Publishing, Inc., P.O. Box 719, Uhrichsville, Ohio 44683, http://www.barbourbooks.com

Member of the
Evangelical Christian
Publishers Association

Illustrations by John Duckworth.

Printed in the United States of America.

SECTION ONE

THE BOOKS OF MOSES

I. IT'S ABOUT TIME

1. Which of the following books of Moses covers the longest time span?

    A. *Exodus*
    B. *Genesis*
    C. *Deuteronomy*
    D. *Judges*
    E. *His daily appointment book*

2. How long did it take to build the Tower of Babel?

    A. *Seven years*
    B. *Four years and two months*
    C. *One score and ten years*
        (thirty years)
    D. *The Bible doesn't say*

3. According to Genesis 1:20-21, what did God create on the fifth day?

    A. *Man*
    B. *Lights (moon and stars)*

C. *Grass, dry land*
D. *Sea creatures and birds*
E. *Labor unions*

4. How old was Noah when the Great Flood
   began?

   A. *120 years*
   B. *600 years*
   C. *247 years*
   D. *300 cubits*

5. Moses' death occurred about:

   A. *3200 B.C.*
   B. *2120 B.C.*
   C. *675 B.C.*
   D. *1405 B.C.*
   E. *Uncertain, as coroner's report is
       incomplete*

6. If a peace offering was made to the Lord, it:

   A. *Could be eaten only that day*
   B. *Could not be eaten at all*
   C. *Could be eaten only that day and the next*

D. *Could only be eaten by the*
   High Priest

7. The book of Numbers begins how long after
   the exodus from Egypt?

   A. *Thirteen months*
   B. *Forty years*
   C. *Four years and five months*
   D. *One hundred three years*
   E. *No one is certain, as the copyright*
      date was washed off in the flood

II. WHO WAS THAT?

1. Whom did God commission to succeed
   Moses in Deuteronomy 31:23?

   A. *Samuel*
   B. *Joshua*
   C. *Ruth*
   D. *Amelek*
   E. *Moses Jr.*
   F. *None of the above*

2. What two people did God say would be spared
   and would enter "the land which I swore I
   would make you dwell in"?

   A. *Moses and Joshua*
   B. *Joshua and Caleb*
   C. *Caleb and Samuel*
   D. *Aaron and Moses*
   E. *Sonny and Cher*

3. Whose sons did God devour with fire for dis-
   obedience?

   A. *Aaron's*
   B. *Moses'*
   C. *"A certain elder's"*
   D. *Uzziel's*
   E. *None of the above*

4. Who built the Ark of the Covenant?

   A. *Uri*
   B. *Hur*
   C. *Aholiab*
   D. *Bezaleel*
   E. *Noah*

5. Whom did God tell Moses He had appeared to in the past?

    A. Abraham, Isaac, and Jacob
    B. Abraham, Noah, and Lot
    C. Adam, Cain, and Abel
    D. Peter, Paul, and Mary

6. Who died in childbirth on the way to Ephrath?

    A. Leah
    B. Bilhah
    C. Rachel
    D. Zilpah
    E. Lot

7. What was the name of Moses' first son?

    A. Isaac
    B. Cain
    C. Reuel
    D. Gershom
    E. None of the above

III. THAT OVER THERE

1. Which of the following was NOT a branch of
   the river that flowed out of Eden?

   A. Hiddekel
   B. Tigris
   C. Gihon
   D. Euphrates
   E. All of these were branches

2. Where was Abraham buried?

   A. Egypt
   B. By the well Lahairoi
   C. Outside the city of Nahor
   D. Shady Lawn Cemetery, just south of
      Tel Aviv
   E. None of the above

3. From what location did Moses view the
   promised land?

   A. A valley in the land of Moab
   B. Mt. Ararat

12

C. The Bible does not say specifically
D. The top of Pisgah
E. The top of the Eiffel Tower

4. What did God tell Moses the western border of the promised land would be?

    A. The Great Sea
    B. The Salt Sea
    C. The Jordan River
    D. Aphek on the south to Tyre on the north
    E. The River Euphrates

5. Balaam is generally best remembered for:

    A. His rod that became a serpent
    B. Slaying Philistines
    C. His craftsmanship with gold
    D. His talking donkey
    E. His flying camel

6. Which of the following were NOT plagues on Egypt?

    A. Darkness
    B. Flies

13

C. Leprosy
D. Lice
E. Locusts
F. Irregularity

7. Which was NOT one of the national feasts
   ordered by God in Exodus 23?

   A. *Feast of the Unleavened Bread*
   B. *Feast of Ingathering*
   C. *Feast of the Covenant*
   D. *Feast of Harvest*

Well, how do you think you did? If you knew
something about each question, your knowledge of
the Mosaic books is definitely above average.

LET'S CHECK THE ANSWERS. . .

THE ANSWERS

SECTION ONE

I. IT'S ABOUT TIME

1. B. The book of Genesis spans roughly 2,300 years—more than all of the other books of the Bible combined. Exodus covers approximately 430 years while Deuteronomy entails only about one month. Judges, the other choice, is NOT a book of Moses. Selection E, Moses' daily appointment book, he soon discovered was not such a good idea. All those stone tablets became extremely heavy, and it was difficult to find the correct tablet for, say, two hundred years from last Tuesday.

2. D. The Bible doesn't say.

3. D. Sea creatures and birds. Man (A) was created on the sixth day, the moon and stars (B) on the fourth day, and the grass and dry land (C) on the third day. Labor unions weren't invented until many years later, although I

often wonder if God sometimes feels over-worked and underpaid.

4. B. Noah was 600 years old when the flood began. Letter A, 120, was Moses' age at his death. Choice C, 247, is how much I anticipate my car insurance premium will be and has nothing to do with scripture. Hopefully, you recognize D, 300 cubits, as the length of the ark. If not, you may want to skip the rest of this section, or the rest of the book for that matter!

5. D. 1405 B.C. The death of Moses is recorded in Deuteronomy 34:5, just after God showed him the promised land.

6. C. The text for this question is Leviticus 19:5–6. Anything that remained the third day was "to be burned in the fire."

7. A. Thirteen months. Choice B, forty years is always a popular alternative for some reason, but it's wrong this time.

II.WHO WAS THAT?

1. B. Joshua. Samuel (A), and Ruth (C),
   weren't born yet. Amelek (D) was detested
   by God (see Deuteronomy 25:17-19). If you
   knew that you don't get bonus points, but pat
   yourself on the back anyway. Since there was
   no Moses Jr. (ever wonder why?) that leaves
   us with Joshua.

2. B. Joshua and Caleb (see Numbers 14:30).
   Moses saw, but never entered the promised
   land, so that rules out A and D (see
   Deuteronomy 34:4). Since Samuel was not
   around at that time (see answer to previous
   question), C is out. That leaves Sonny and
   Cher, a husband and wife (long since
   divorced) singing duo from the 60's. But
   that's the 1960's. THE A.D. 1960's!!!

3. A. Aaron's (see Leviticus 10:1-2). Little is
   said about Moses after his return to Egypt.
   Letter C, "a certain elder" sounded like a
   convincing answer, or a good guess. D,
   Uzziel, appears in Exodus 6:18-22 as the son
   of Kohath. But then, you probably already
   knew that.

4. D. Bezaleel. Now that Indiana Jones has renewed everyone's interest in the ark, it's only right that you should know who built it! . . .Uri (A) was Bezaleel's father, while (B), Hur, was his grandfather. (Clever, huh!) Letter C, Aholiab, was also an artisan who worked on the sanctuary (see Exodus chapter 36), but the Bible makes no mention of his working on the ark. As for choice E, Noah, yes he did build an ark, but his was for carrying people, not tablets. The people in the ark carried their own tablets. . .probably Dramamine.

5. A. Specifically those three in Exodus 6:3. As for the other choices, Lot, Adam, and Cain were all men who had disappointed God, thus eliminating B and C. Peter, Paul and Mary (D) although all Bible names, are best remembered for *Puff the Magic Dragon.*

6. C. Rachel (see Genesis 35:18-19). Leah (A) was Rachel's older sister and also Jacob's wife (another story), while Bilhah (B) was Rachel's maidservant. Zilpah (D) was Leah's maidservant. Although Lot (choice E) lived in a place where homosexuality was

rampant, to the best of our knowledge, he never became pregnant.

7. D. Gershom (see Exodus 2:22). Isaac, of course, was the son of Abraham, and Cain was Adam's son. Reuel was Moses' father-in-law (see Exodus 2:18-21).

III. THAT OVER THERE

1. B. While the Tigris is not far away, it is not mentioned in this text. See Genesis 2:10-14.

2. E. None of the above. The scriptures tell us in Genesis 25:9-10 Abraham was buried in the cave of Machpelah, which is before Mamre, in the field of Ephron. (A) Egypt? Nope. Abraham (Abram) spent some time there back in chapter twelve, but he didn't stay long. B? Sorry. Lahairoi was where Isaac lived after Abraham's death. C, the city of Nahor in Mesopotamia, is where Abraham sent his servant to find a wife for Isaac. As for choice D, Abraham might have considered Tel Aviv a nice place to visit—but he wouldn't have wanted to die there.

3. Well, since it's generally difficult to view very much from a valley, that rules out A. Mt. Ararat (B) is where Noah's ark finally settled. Since the Bible DOES tell us, forget C, also. That leaves us with either the Eiffel Tower or the top of Pisgah. If you still can't decide, refer to Deuteronomy 34:1 (or maybe take a nap).

4. A. The Great Sea (see Numbers 34:6). Today we know it as the Mediterranean. The Salt Sea (now known as the Dead Sea) was part of the southeastern boundary. The River Jordan was part of the eastern border. Letter D, Aphek to Tyre, would be close, but would not go all the way to the sea. E, the River Euphrates is far to the east. It runs from the Black Sea to the Persian Gulf. Isn't it amazing what you're learning so far? I don't think so either.

5. D. I would imagine that you've heard of Balaam's talking donkey (more specifically it was the Lord speaking through the donkey), but if you hadn't, you have now!! Moses was the one whose rod became a serpent (A), and Samson (B) was adept at slaying Philistines (with a donkey's jaw—who knows, maybe Balaam's donkey's jaw). C was a trick answer which probably fooled no one. E, "flying camel?" See Big Time Wrestling!!!

6. C and F. Darkness (A) was the ninth plague (see Exodus 10:21-23). Flies (B) were the fourth plague (see Exodus 8:21). Lice (D) were the third plague (see Exodus 8:16-18). Locusts were the eighth plague (see Exodus 10:12–15). Leprosy, choice C, was not a plague but rather a disease which was much misunderstood in Bible times, and was thought to be contagious. Concerning F, God did not send irregularity upon Pharaoh, although most everyone since has been plagued by it at one time or another!

7. C. Feast of the Covenant. The feasts of the unleavened bread, harvest, and ingathering, respectively, were commanded by God in Exodus 23:14-16. To the best of my knowledge (which admittedly is not saying much), there was not a Feast of the Covenant. Seems to me there was no happy medium in the Old Testament. It was either feast or famine.

Section one is now history. But I guess it has been for quite some time! But let's get serious for a minute or so because it's time for your score. There were twenty-one questions, and if you wish you may write your score here.

TOTAL CORRECT ANSWERS: _____

SCORE
EVALUATION

21-19: Wow! If you did that well, you may know more about the books of Moses than Moses! I probably wouldn't score that high myself—which is rather sad when you consider that I wrote the questions.

18-14: This is an excellent score unless you happen to be a theologian or an Old Testament afficionado, in which case it's simply a "good" score.

13-10: Don't be alarmed or disappointed if you rated in this category. Eleven through thirteen correct is still above fifty percent. . .but not much.

9-5: Fair. (I'm being diplomatic.) Look on the bright side—this is the only section of this book that has these questions. The other sections have different questions. Now do you feel better?

4-0: Oops! Your hope may lie in the fact that the Second Coming may take place before you finish this book. But charge ahead anyway!

RIGHT THIS WAY. . .

SECTION TWO

THE TWELVE HISTORICAL BOOKS

I. It Happened Here

1. According to Joshua, chapter three, what body of water did God cause to be separated so that the people could cross?

    A. The Sea of Galilee
    B. The Red Sea
    C. The Jordan River
    D. The Tigris
    E. Lake Jericho

2. What city suffered greatly for having the Ark of the Covenant in its possession?

    A. Ebenezer
    B. Ashdod
    C. Dagon
    D. Jerusalem
    E. Butte, Montana

3. What did David conquer immediately after becoming king of Israel?

    A. Judah
    B. Ishbosheth

C. Tyre
D. Syria
E. His fear of public speaking
F. None of the above

4. According to 2 Kings the destruction and captivity of Israel in 722 B. C. was brought about by what nation?

A. Assyria
B. Egypt
C. Babylon
D. Judah
E. Mexico

5. The book of 2 Chronicles focuses on this country.

A. Babylon
B. Israel
C. Persia
D. Judah
E. None of the above

6. Nehemiah served here before leaving for Jerusalem.

    A. *In Babylonian government*
    B. *In the Persian palace*
    C. *As a royal priest in Syria*
    D. *In Ethiopia, as a historian*
    E. *In Venice, as a gondolier*

7. What country did Ishbosheth rule for two years?

    A. *Philistia*
    B. *Syria*
    C. *Israel*
    D. *Tyre*
    E. *Rim (for the "Tyre" of course)*

II.OLD (TESTAMENT) FOLKS AT HOME

1. Although Esther was a Jew, she became:

    A. *An attendant of Queen Vashti*
    B. *The Queen of Sheba*

C. *The wife of Nehemiah*
D. *The Queen of Persia*
E. *A Gentile*

2. What was unique about Joash, King of Judah?

   A. *He had only one arm*
   B. *He was a eunuch*
   C. *He was an orphan*
   D. *He was a mighty warrior*
   E. *He was only seven years old*

3. In 2 Kings chapter two, how was Elijah transported to Heaven?

   A. *In a cloud*
   B. *He climbed a golden ladder*
   C. *In a whirlwind*
   D. *He ascended with no visible means*
   E. *In the space shuttle*

4. What happened to the youths who mocked Elisha on his way to Bethel, after he pronounced a curse on them?

    A. *They fell dead instantly*
    B. *They were mauled by bears*
    C. *They were struck by lightning*
    D. *They were turned to stone*
    E. *Nothing*

5. David and Bathsheba's second child was named. . .

    A. *Solomon*
    B. *Absalom*
    C. *Amnon*
    D. *Tamar*
    E. *Ralph*

6. Whom did Saul consult at En Dor?

    A. *A physician*
    B. *David*
    C. *The King of Gath*
    D. *A medium*
    E. *A financial planner*

7. Who was spared at Jericho by Joshua?

    A. *Women and children*
    B. *Rahab the harlot, and her*
       family
    C. *Achan, the son of Carmi*
    D. *Oxen, sheep and donkeys*
    E. *All who cried "uncle"*

III. IT'S A MIRACLE
(AMAZING OCCURRENCES)

1. How did Elisha help the widow pay her debt?

    A. *By causing her creditors*
       to forget
    B. *By turning her silver into*
       gold
    C. *By increasing her oil*
    D. *By creating money from*
       nothing
    E. *By renegotiating her loans*
       and co-signing a note for her

2. What miracle did Elisha perform while he and his men were cutting trees to build a dwelling near the Jordan?

   A. *He made an axe head float*
   B. *He restored a hewn down tree*
   C. *He restored life to a man who had been crushed to death by a falling tree*
   D. *He made the hardwoods so soft that they were easily cut*
   E. *He produced a McCullogh chain saw from under his garment*

3. The first Passover celebrated in the promised land was followed the next day by what divine act?

   A. *The walls of Jericho fell*
   B. *Abraham appeared to Joshua in a dream*
   C. *Music came from the Ark of the Covenant*
   D. *God stopped providing manna*

4. What happened to the angel who foretold Samson's birth to his parents, when they offered a sacrifice to God?

    A. *He became as stone*
    B. *He blew upon the fire and put it out*
    C. *He ascended in the flame of the altar*
    D. *He reproved them*
    E. *He sang, "Is your all on the altar"*

5. What miracle took place after the Ark of the Covenant was brought to Solomon's temple?

    A. *The ark floated in the air*
    B. *A cloud filled the temple*
    C. *The priests were struck silent*
    D. *Solomon's robe was turned white*
    E. *Property taxes were reduced*

6. How was Elijah fed during the drought in Israel according to 1 Kings 17:4-6?

    A. *Manna from Heaven*
    B. *God sent a donkey carrying food*
    C. *He drank water from a brook,*
       and fasted
    D. *Ravens brought him food twice*
       a day
    E. *He ate at "Colonel Ahab's*
       Samarian Fried Chicken"

7. Before Samson told Delilah what would truly cause him to lose his miraculous strength, he told her three lies. Which of the following is NOT one of the lies?

    A. *Weaving his seven locks into the*
       web of a loom
    B. *Putting out his eyes*
    C. *Binding him with seven fresh bow*
       strings
    D. *Binding him securely with new ropes*

Congratulations! You're now finished with Section Two. But wait. . .maybe these congratulations are a bit premature. Let's see how you did.

LE ANSWA
(Okay—so I ain't much on French)

Section Two

I. It Happened Here

1. C. The Jordan River. Choice A, the Sea of
   Galilee, was known at that time as the Sea
   of Chinnereth, and had little known significance until Christ's time. The Red Sea (B)
   was parted by God for Moses and the
   Israelites, but that was many years earlier
   (probably forty, give or take). The Tigris is
   too far east, and Lake Jericho (E) sounds like
   a good place to buy a condo, but I doubt
   Joshua was much of a water-skier.

2. B. Ashdod. The Philistines soon found that
   the Ark of the Covenant did not go with their
   decor—specifically their idol "Dagon" (C).
   After God destroyed their idol, he gave them
   tumors (probably bubonic plague) and they
   hastily sent the ark on its way (see 1 Samuel
   5–6). Ebenezer (A) was where they brought

the ark FROM. The ark eventually made it to Jerusalem (D), with God's blessing. If you happen to be fond of Butte, Montana (E), please don't take it seriously. I was trying to come up with an "off-the-wall" choice, and this one turned out to be a Butte.

3. F. None of the above. The correct answer here would be Jerusalem. Shortly after David's anointing as king of Israel at age thirty, his conquest of Jerusalem took place (see 2 Samuel 5). David was already king of Judah (A), and Ishbosheth (B) was not a country but rather Saul's son who had been killed earlier. David formed an alliance with Tyre (C), and did defeat Syria (D), but not until sometime later after several other battles had occurred. The Bible doesn't mention anything about David having a fear of public speaking (E), and considering what happened to Goliath, I doubt that anyone would have laughed if they heard King David stutter—at least not out loud anyway.

4. A. Assyria. After being led by nineteen con-secutive evil kings, Israel fell to the Assyrians in 722 B. C. The Egyptians (B) were busy defending themselves in a lawsuit over a pyramid scheme, while Babylon (C) was

eyeing Judah (D) which it conquered about 136 years later. Mexico (E) was not into conquering other nations at that time. They were attempting to go high-tech, but ended up settling for Az-tec.

5. D. Judah. The Book of 2 Chronicles focuses on Judah, and especially on its godly kings. Israel (B) is basically ignored because of its false worship and ungodly rulers.

6. B. Nehemiah served as a "cupbearer" (see Nehemiah 1:11). He probably was responsible for tasting the king's wine, to make sure it wasn't poisoned. The hours were good, and the work wasn't too difficult—it was just the "on-the-job-training" that killed you.

7. C. Saul's son, Ishbosheth, ruled Israel for just two years. A, Philistia, was Samson's territory (see Judges). Syria (B) was too far north and probably out of Israel's control during that time. As for D and E—sorry—I couldn't resist.

II. OLD (TESTAMENT) FOLKS AT HOME

1. D. Esther became the Queen of Persia as a result of Queen Vashti's (see A) refusal to show up for the king's gala. As far as we know (?) Nehemiah wasn't married, ruling out C. The Queen of Sheba (B) is mentioned in 1 Kings 10:1-13, concerning a visit to Solomon. Choice E is just not Kosher—at all.

2. E. He was only seven years old (see 2 Chronicles 24:1). He was probably the only kid in history who had "real" soldiers to play with.

3. C. In a whirlwind. While clouds (A) were prevalent during Old Testament times, God chose not to use one on this occasion. A golden ladder (B) would have been unique, but Jacob cornered the ladder market (see Genesis 28:10-13). D, ascending with no visible means, was done later by Christ. What about selection E? No, Elijah never rode in the space shuttle. Said he just didn't feel comfortable with the "O" rings.

4. Letter A, falling dead instantly, is usually

attributable to Ananias and Sapphira for their deceit in Acts 5. Letter C, struck by lightning, is for overzealous golfers. D, turning to stone, would be similar to Lot's wife, except she became "rock salt." Did her husband then become a "vacant Lot"??? Yes—the answer is B, they were mauled by bears. The funny thing was, they weren't anywhere near Chicago. Reference: 2 Kings 2:24.

5. A. Solomon was David and Bathsheba's second child. You may recall that Absalom (B) and Amnon (C) were also David's sons, the latter committing incest with Tamar (D). Actually King David liked the name Ralph (E), but Bathsheba just wouldn't go for it.

6. Actually, Saul went to En Dor looking for a small or a large, but he couldn't find either, so he ended up with a medium, D.

7. B. Rahab the harlot and her family were spared (see Joshua 6:25). Rahab was responsible for protecting Joshua's spies sent to scout Jericho, and she was spared in return for her help. Many of the people of Jericho tried saying "uncle"—but to no avail. What they should have said was "I'm Rahab's uncle!"

III. It's A Miracle

1. C. Increasing her oil (see 2 Kings 4:1-7). The Saudi-Arabians have become quite good at this also in recent years. A—No, creditors don't forget. B—Alchemy, hasn't worked yet. D—Counterfeiting, illegal. E—What the rest of us end up doing.

2. A. He made an axe head float. Were any of the other answers convincing? If you chose E, you definitely have a problem. See your pastor—or your psychiatrist.

3. Reread the question. When God STOPS doing something, that is also a divine act. See Joshua 5:12 for reference.

4. C. The angel ascended in the flame of the altar (see Judges 13:20).

5. The Bible tells of no instance where the ark floats in the air (A). Nor am I aware of priests being struck silent (C). Solomon's robe never changed colors (unless of course, he washed it without following the label instructions). And letter E, reducing property

taxes—now that would REALLY be a miracle wouldn't it! Answer B (see 2 Chronicles 5:13).

6. Manna from Heaven (A) was fed to the children of Israel on their journey to the promised land. B is also incorrect, although donkeys have had a significant role in the Bible. C is partially right—he did drink from a brook, but he didn't fast. (Drinking fast can give you the hiccups.) As a footnote, legend has it that as Elijah was leaving that place he asked the ravens when they might feed him again—only to hear them reply "Nevermore." P.S. The answer is D if you haven't already ascertained that information.

7. Judges 16:7-17 tells us the story of how Samson fabricated tales in order to "tease" Delilah. A, C, and D were all true. Samson later did have his eyes gouged out. It was done by a couple of men from the business community, where "gouging" is a way of life. One question you may have asked yourself about this story is, "I wonder if all those Philistines who were killed when Samson collapsed the temple had life insurance?" And it is a good question. The answer is yes—they were all covered.

* * * * *

You have now completed scoring for Section Two and should be gaining vast Biblical knowledge, or approaching a nervous breakdown. But be of good cheer. Besides, you bought this book of your own free will and therefore have only yourself to blame. Now do you feel better? Neither do I.

TOTAL CORRECT ANSWERS: _____

PLEASE SEE NEXT PAGE FOR SECTION TWO SCORING EVALUATION.

SCORE EVALUATION

21–20: The only way you could achieve this score is by being a genius, a liar, or a cheater. And since I have no use for any of the above, I will not comment further.

19–16: This is an excellent score considering this is a part of the Bible that most folks don't read often. Pat yourself on the back with a donkey's jawbone.

15–12: Respectable. If you laughed at most of the jokes, I'll give you a B plus.

11–8: Average. You could hit almost that many by guessing. And my guess is that you did.

7–0: This score qualifies you to write the sequel to this book!

DON'T STOP NOW. . .
YOU'RE ALREADY IN TOO DEEP!!!!

SECTION
THREE

Patience, Praise,
and Poetry

I. When Rotten Things Happen to Godly People

1. Which of the following were not part of Satan's first assault on Job?

    A. *His oxen and donkeys were stolen*
    B. *His body became covered with sores*
    C. *His servants were killed*
    D. *His sons were killed*
    E. *He discovered a hole in his favorite jeans*

2. What was Job's wife's advice to him after Satan's second assault?

    A. *Worship God in all things*
    B. *God is punishing you for your sin—repent*
    C. *Give all you have to the poor*
    D. *Curse God and die*
    E. *Get more life insurance*

3. Which of the following was part of Job's reward for having suffered adversity?

    A. *He had more gold than anyone in the land*

    B. *He lived longer than anyone in his family*

    C. *His daughters were the most beautiful*

    D. *He accumulated more land than anyone*

    E. *His stock portfolio outperformed the Dow Jones industrial averages*

4. The 51st Psalm is of special significance because it is. . .

    A. *A psalm of repentance after David's sin of adultery*

    B. *David's first psalm celebrating becoming King of Israel*

    C. *A psalm commemorating David's deliverance from Saul*

    D. *The only psalm not written by David*

    E. *In celebration of the grand opening of Israel's first K-Mart store*

5. According to Proverbs 24:16, how many times can a righteous man fall, and still rise up again?

   A. *Seventy times seven*
   B. *Seven*
   C. *Many*
   D. *Forty*
   E. *It depends on how coordinated he is*

6. In chapter three of Ecclesiastes, which of the following does the author say there is a time and a season for?

   A. *Planting*
   B. *Dancing*
   C. *Feasting*
   D. *Singing*
   E. *Hating*
   F. *Laughing*
   G. *Reading poorly written books*

7. In Song of Solomon, what happened twice to the Shulamite woman?

    A. *She was punished for not keeping the vineyards*
    B. *She was struck by the watchmen of the city*
    C. *She had a dream of separation from her lover*
    D. *She was chastised by her brothers*
    E. *She lost two games of "Solomon says"*

II. "NAMEDROPPERS" (WHODUNIT?)

1. Which of the following was NOT one of the men who debated with Job during his suffering?

    A. *Eliphaz*
    B. *Hezekiah*
    C. *Bildad (but don't expect him to pay you)*
    D. *Zophar (zogood) (Get it? Zophar-zogood!)*
    E. *Al*

2. Select the names of Job's three daughters
   from the following:

   A. Jemima
   B. Kezia
   C. Elihu
   D. Tamar
   E. Mahlah
   F. Kerenhappuch
   G. Jobetta

3. Which of the following did NOT write a
   psalm?

   A. David
   B. Solomon
   C. Moses
   D. Ethan
   E. All of the above wrote at least one

4. What godly predecessor did David name in
   Psalm 14?

   A. Jacob
   B. Abraham
   C. Noah
   D. Paul
   E. George Burns

5. Proverbs 31 was written by. . .

    A. *Solomon*
    B. *Hezekiah*
    C. *David*
    D. *King Lemuel*
    E. *The Shulamite woman*

6. The "preacher" in Ecclesiastes is generally thought to be. . .

    A. *Jonah*
    B. *Isaiah*
    C. *Solomon*
    D. *Jeremiah*
    E. *Billy Graham, Minneapolis,*
       Minnesota

7. The Shulamite woman from Song of Solomon was a. . .

    A. *Maker of cloth*
    B. *Vineyard keeper*
    C. *Seller of fruit in the marketplace*
    D. *Tribal dancer*
    E. *Hat check girl at the Hilton*

III. Are You Kidding?
(interesting facts)

1. In Job chapter one, what was Satan's reply when God asked him where he had been?

   A. *"In Hades counting my souls"*
   B. *"Hiding in a cave"*
   C. *"Going to and fro in the earth"*
   D. *"Searching the earth for followers"*
   E. *"Who wants to know?"*

2. Which of Job's possessions were the same in number after his suffering as they were prior to it?

   A. *His sons and daughters*
   B. *Sheep*
   C. *Camels*
   D. *Oxen*
   E. *His baseball card collection*

3. The word "selah" is used seventy-one times in the Psalms, and probably means:

   A. *"Let it be so"*
   B. *"Praise to Almighty God"*
   C. *A musical crescendo, or pause*
   D. *Written by King David*
   E. *To be continued*

4. According to Proverbs 22, what is rather to be chosen than great riches?

   A. *Friendship with God*
   B. *A good name*
   C. *A pure wife*
   D. *Wisdom*
   E. *A government job*

5. While "the preacher" of Ecclesiastes states that "all is vanity," his final conclusion is:

   A. *Righteousness is its own reward*
   B. *Do your best in everything you do*
   C. *Enjoy your short, vain life*
   D. *Fear God and keep His commandments*
   E. *Never putt with a nine iron*

6. Some theologians question how Solomon could record his love for the Shulamite woman in Song of Solomon since he had at that time a harem of:

    A. *One hundred forty women*
    B. *Twenty-four women*
    C. *Eight women*
    D. *Well over one thousand women*
    E. *None of the above—Solomon always had trouble attracting women*

7. In chapter seven of Song of Solomon, to what does Solomon compare the Shulamite woman's nose?

    A. *The nose of a gazelle*
    B. *A fawn*
    C. *A beautiful jewel*
    D. *A banana*
    E. *The Tower of Lebanon*

BOY, ARE YOU GLAD THIS IS OVER?
ME TOO.

DA
SOLUTIONS

SECTION THREE

I. WHEN ROTTEN THINGS HAPPEN TO GODLY PEOPLE
(EXAMPLE: YOU—READING THIS BOOK.)

1. B. Satan's first attack on Job is recorded in Job 1:13-22. Satan was instructed by God not to lay a hand on Job's body. Choice E is incorrect, because Job had some very well-made jeans. They were made by the third son of Jacob and Leah (see Genesis 29:34).

2. Job's wife would never have made it as a Sunday School teacher or church pianist. She told Job, "Curse God and die" (D) (see Job 2:9).

3. C. Job's daughters were the most beautiful in all the land (see Job 42:15). He also

accumulated more wealth, but nothing else offered as choices is specifically mentioned in the Bible. As far as his stock portfolio (E), old Job never was much good at the stock market. He always bought on margin and tried to make a quick killing, and usually failed. His broker always told Job he just didn't have enough patience.

4. A. David asked for forgiveness after his sin of adultery in Psalm 51. David's celebration of becoming king (B) is most likely Psalm 2. Psalm 18 was written upon David's deliverance from Saul (C), and since David only wrote about half the Psalms, that rules out D. David declined to write a Psalm for the grand opening of Israel's first K-Mart store (E). He did, however, get on the microphone and say, "Attention K-Mart shoppers, all slings in our sporting goods department are now thirty percent off!" It was a Goliath sale. (Sorry.)

5. B. Seven. Seven is a number used often in the Bible, so it's a good choice if you're uncertain. You should recognize A as the amount of times Christ told us to forgive one another (see Matthew 18:22; as you read this book please keep that in mind). Choice C, many, is also a logical idea, but it's also a wrong answer.

Letter D, forty, is also used many times (flood, fasting, and so on). Since this verse is intended in the spiritual sense, do not encourage me to discuss choice E. I just couldn't help it. Pray for me.

6. Solomon's "time for every purpose" soliloquy has always been a personal favorite of mine, and I couldn't resist putting in a question about it. Correct answers are: A, B, E, and F. Feasting, singing, and reading poorly written books were not on the preacher's list.

7. C. She had a dream of separation from her lover. Solomon should have told her that eating too much before you go to bed produces bad dreams. I guess even Solomon didn't know everything.

II. NAMEDROPPERS

1. B. Hezekiah was the King of Judah (see 2 Chronicles 29:1-3). Al (E), didn't show up either. In fact, Al doesn't show up at all in the Bible. You just can't count on some people. (As Job found out.)

2. Job's three daughters were: A, Jemima, B, Kezia, and F, Kerenhappuch. Reference is Job 42:14. Elihu (C) was a man who debated with Job (see Job 32). Tamar (D) you may recall from 2 Samuel 13, and Mahlah (E) is found in Numbers 27:1. Choice G, "Jobetta," has a certain ring to it for a girl whose father's name was Job, but—well—er—ah forget it!

3. E. All of these people wrote at least one psalm. Surprised? Me too!

4. A. Psalm 14 is significant for its beginning, "The fool hath said in his heart. . ." and verse seven says "Let Jacob rejoice." Paul, selection D, hadn't been born yet, so that pretty much takes him out of the picture. Choice E, George Burns, only PLAYED God, and we must be careful for we sometimes do, too.

5. D. King Lemuel. While Solomon (A) was the chief contributor to Proverbs, he also collected the sayings of others (see Ecclesiastes 12:9). Hezekiah (B) had his scribes copy and organize some of Solomon's work (see Proverbs 25:1). David (C) was the main author of Psalms, and the Shulamite woman (E) was Solomon's wife. (E pluribus unum.)

6. C. Solomon. Too easy? Maybe. If you chose A, Jonah, you were probably just fishing for an answer, and I can't really say you did a whale of a job, because it's the wrong answer. (Puns are my life—too bad, huh?) Isaiah (B), and Jeremiah (D), were both major prophets (which is not to be confused with what the oil companies show on their balance sheets every year), and while E, Billy Graham, Minneapolis, Minnesota, is certainly an excellent evangelist, he's not "the preacher."

7. B. Vineyard keeper (see Song of Solomon 1:6). Since I've now referred to the Shulamite twice, you may be beginning to think I have a special interest in her, and I have to admit that I do. You see, Solomon and I have three things in common: a special interest in the Shulamite woman, faith in God, and extraordinary wisdom. Well. . .two out of three ain't bad.

III. ARE YOU KIDDING?

1. C. See Job 1:7. Even Satan knows how far he can go, and chances are if E were correct, God wouldn't have waited 'til the "latter days" to finish old Beelzebub off.

2. A. Sons and daughters. While the "double blessing" often referred to does apply to Job's livestock (B, C, and D), he ended up with seven sons and three daughters (see Job 42:13). God never did restore Job's baseball card collection. Job really only missed one card, Job DiMaggio, but he still thought God was tops.

3. C. Selah was most likely a musical term—possibly a crescendo or pause. Choice A would be the definition of "amen" and E, to be continued, was seldom used in those days. People had more time on their hands to hear the Psalms in their entirety, and I just can't fathom King David saying, "Come back next week—same time, same temple!"

4. While A, C, D, and E are all nice to have, a good name (B) is correct. While it is very possible to have friendship with God and a good name and a pure wife, I'm uncertain if you can have both wisdom and a government job! (Just kidding, I.R.S. agents!)

5. D. Fear God and keep His commandments (see Ecclesiastes 12:13). I don't know if Solomon ever tried putting with a nine iron (E), but I'll guarantee you he saw his share of sand traps!

6. A. 140 women. Song of Solomon 6:8 states that Solomon had sixty queens and eighty concubines. (I always thought a concubine was farm machinery!)

7. E. I guess it was meant to be a compliment, but in Song of Solomon 7:4, Solomon describes the Shulamite woman's nose as "like the Tower of Lebanon." Choice D, "a banana," was something I happened to remember from the old Danny Thomas show!

You have now conquered the third section, and it's time to check your score. (And maybe your blood pressure.)

TOTAL CORRECT ANSWERS: _____

SCORING EVALUATION

21-19: Amazing—simply amazing. Not your score, but the fact that anyone so knowledgeable hasn't thrown away this book by now!

18-15: Very good! But remember it's not necessarily what you know, but what you DON'T know that can get you.

14-11: Respectable. At least by people who score BELOW this level!

10-7: Look how much you've learned! You've learned (at least) that there are also others who need to sharpen their Biblical knowledge . . .like the author.

6-0: We've talked before, haven't we?

SECTION
FOUR

Never Turn Down
a Prophet

I. Prophetable Information to Know

1. This prophet is often referred to as "the Shakespeare of the prophets."

    A. *Daniel*
    B. *Jeremiah*
    C. *Ezekiel*
    D. *Isaiah*
    E. *Habakkuk*

2. This prophet was commended three times by his contemporary, Ezekiel, for his righteousness.

    A. *Isaiah*
    B. *Daniel*
    C. *Jeremiah*
    D. *Zephaniah*
    E. *Lamentations*

3. Tradition holds that Isaiah died as a result of:

    A. *Stoning*
    B. *Being sawed in two*

C. *The plague (probably bubonic)*
D. *Dropsy, a heart disease*
E. *In an auto accident*

4. Which of the following is NOT true concerning Jeremiah?

   A. *He was the son of King Jehoiakim*
   B. *The Lord told him not to marry*
   C. *He was put in stocks and publicly humiliated*
   D. *He preached and prophesied for more than forty years*
   E. *He was a bullfrog*

5. Ezekiel's ministry took place when Judah was in captivity under what nation?

   A. *Tyre*
   B. *Babylon*
   C. *Philistia*
   D. *Egypt*
   E. *Great Britain*

6. Who was king of Babylon when Daniel was put in the lion's den?

   A. *Jehoiakim*
   B. *Nebuchadnezzar*
   C. *Darius*
   D. *Belshazzar*
   E. *King Tut*

7. Jeremiah prophesied during:

   A. *The peak of Judah's prosperity*
   B. *Judah's darkest hours just before its captivity*
   C. *The time when Judah was coming out of Babylonian captivity*
   D. *The depths of Judah's captivity*
   E. *Half time of Judah's basketball games*

II. "PROPHET AND LOSS"
(PREDICTIONS OF THE PROPHETS)

1. In the first ten chapters of Isaiah, three nations have judgments against them prophesied. They are:

   A. *Babylon, Philistia, and Tyre*
   B. *Egypt, Babylon, and Assyria*
   C. *Judah, Egypt, and Arabia*
   D. *Judah, Israel, and Assyria*
   E. *Austria, Switzerland, and Siberia*

2. In the first chapter of Isaiah, what did Isaiah say Judah would have been comparable to, had not the Lord left a small remnant?

   A. *The land of Noah after the flood*
   B. *Sodom and Gomorrah*
   C. *The children of Israel dying in the wilderness*
   D. *The land of Egypt during God's judgment of Pharaoh*
   E. *A house without carpeting*

3. Jeremiah's first prophecy to Judah was concerning its sin of:

   A. Adultery
   B. Homosexuality
   C. Idolatry
   D. Greed
   E. Jaywalking

4. Ezekiel prophesied the downfall of many
Gentile nations but spent the most time discussing which of the following:

   A. Sidon
   B. Tyre
   C. Philistia
   D. Moab
   E. Mozambique

5. Which of the following is NOT part of
Ezekiel's prophetic claims concerning the
restoration of Israel?

   A. God appointed Ezekiel as a watchman
   B. The valley of dry bones
   C. The handwriting on the wall
   D. The new temple

6. Daniel's first recorded prophecy was an interpretation of a dream concerning:

    A. *A feast given by Belshazzar*
    B. *The kingdoms following Nebuchadnezzar*
    C. *Four beasts rising from the sea*
    D. *A ram standing beside a river*
    E. *A Ford Pinto exploding when struck from behind*

7. In Daniel's final recorded prophecy, what did the "man in linen" reply when Daniel asked "What shall be the end of these things?"

    A. *"The words are closed up and sealed till the time of the end"*
    B. *"The abomination of desolation"*
    C. *"The elements shall melt with fervent heat"*
    D. *"The Son of God shall descend with a shout"*
    E. *"The Detroit Lions will actually have a winning season"*

III. For Spiritual Prophet...
(God's teachings through His prophets)

1. "Come now and let us reason together," says the Lord, "though your sins be as scarlet, they shall be as white as snow." This scripture is found in the Book of

    A. Jeremiah
    B. Daniel
    C. Ezekiel
    D. Lamentations
    E. None of the above

2. God gave this prophet a scroll and told him to eat it, and it was "in my mouth like honey for sweetness."

    A. Ezekiel
    B. Isaiah
    C. Jeremiah
    D. Daniel
    E. Kevin

3. "Thou art weighed in the balances, and art found wanting. . ." was God's judgment given to. . .

  A. Ezekiel concerning Judah
  B. Isaiah concerning Babylon
  C. Jeremiah concerning King Jehoiakim
  D. Daniel concerning Belshazzar
  E. Zacchaeus concerning his small size

4. When Christ referred to the temple full of moneychangers and dove sellers as a "den of thieves," he was paraphrasing which of the following prophets?

  A. Daniel
  B. Isaiah
  C. Jeremiah
  D. Ezekiel
  E. Paul

5. What did the Lord tell Ezekiel the "army" of dry bones represented?

  A. "All My enemies"
  B. "Eternal death for sin"
  C. "The whole house of Israel"

D. *"The nations who profaned My name"*
   E. *"People who eat health food"*

6. The "New Covenant" (I will be their God, and
   they shall be My people) was given through
   this prophet.

   A. *Daniel*
   B. *Jeremiah*
   C. *Ezekiel*
   D. *Isaiah*
   E. *None of the above*

7. In Isaiah 59, what two things did God say
   would not depart from His people, or their
   descendants, "from henceforth and for ever"?

   A. *"My laws and My sabbaths"*
   B. *"My holiness and My word"*
   C. *"My righteousness and My vengeance"*
   D. *"My spirit and My words"*
   E. *"My Triple A guide to Jerusalem and
       My chicken soup recipe"*

WOW. . .ARE WE GLAD THIS ONE IS OVER!?

CORRECTO CHOICE-O'S

SECTION FOUR

I. PROPHETABLE INFORMATION TO KNOW

1. D. Isaiah, because of his style of writing and attention to detail, is often referred to as "the Shakespeare of the prophets." That is not to say that the others listed here are not important. Habakkuk, for example, is often referred to as "that guy with three k's in his name."

2. B. Daniel—one of the most highly esteemed prophets—was "greatly beloved" (see Daniel 9:23). Just in case you didn't know, E, Lamentations, was not a prophet, but rather Jeremiah's sorrowful writing about the fall of Jerusalem in 586 B.C.

3. B. Tradition says that Isaiah was sawed in two by his persecutors during Manassah's

rule. What a way to go! Choice D, dropsy the heart disease, is one I suffer from. It's where you drop on your duff and don't have the heart to get up. Also, concerning choice E, auto accidents were rare in Isaiah's day. They became more prevalent, however, after King Hezekiah issued a decree in 710 B.C. allowing a right turn on red.

4. A. (Also E. It was almost too cheap and obvious to put in there. . .but I'd already come this far). Jeremiah was the son of Hilkiah, a priest (see Jeremiah 1:1).

5. B. Babylon. Tyre and Philistia (A, C) were both eventually taken by Babylon also. Egypt (D) is dealt with harshly in Ezekiel chapters 29-32, and 29:15 states "it shall be the basest of the kingdoms."

6. C. Nebuchadnezzar (B) had been "put out to pasture" and his son Belshazzar had been killed. Actually, King Jehoiakim considered himself to be a lot like King Tut (E). Finally one day his wife said to him, "C'mon—what've you and Tut in common?"

7. B. Jeremiah prophesied just prior to the fall of Judah to Babylon. While choice D may seem

partially correct, that is not the case. He did not prophesy after Judah's fall, but did minister in Jerusalem and Egypt for about six years.

II. Prophet and Loss

1. D. While all of the nations mentioned in A, B, and C had judgments prophesied against them by Isaiah, only Israel, Judah and Assyria were dealt with in the first ten chapters. God has judged Austria and Switzerland (E) to be nice vacation spots, and Siberia, while not exactly a Mecca for tourists, still has many people living there by choice. Unfortunately, it's not *their* choice.

2. B. Sodom and Gomorrah. Isaiah compared Judah's coming fate to those cities in verses nine and ten. Choice E is significant because even though carpet is not mentioned in the Bible, we do know that God left Judah a small remnant.

3. C. Jeremiah began reproving Judah for its idolatry, and compared the nation to a harlot (see Jeremiah 2:5, 3:1). While it's likely that adultery (A), homosexuality (B), and greed (D)

were also common, choice E, jaywalking, hadn't been considered a misdemeanor, let alone a sin. You see, the mode of transportation at that time was either by chariot, which was pulled by an animal, or riding on the back of an animal, or walking. Now, we all know what animals do in the road. Therefore, walking in a straight line to cross the street was almost certain to ruin your best sandals. I'll bet you never thought of that before. . . I'll bet you wish I hadn't either.

4. B. Ezekiel spent more time discussing Tyre, a city which still exists today on the Mediterranean Sea in southern Lebanon. Many theologians believe that the ruler of Tyre in Ezekiel's day was actually Satan himself! Alternative answers Sidon, Philistia, and Moab were all included by Ezekiel, but he never mentioned Mozambique. You see, Ezekiel had a simple rule that he lived by. It was, "never prophesy against a country whose name you can't spell."

5. C. You will recall that the handwriting on the wall is from Daniel chapter five. Ezekiel was appointed a watchman (Ezekiel 33:7), the valley of dry bones (B) is discussed in Ezekiel 37, and the new temple (D) is found in Ezekiel chapter 40.

6. B. See Daniel 2:31-35. The feast given by Belshazzar led to the writing on the wall (see Daniel 5:5). The four beasts (C) was Daniel's own dream, which is recorded in chapter seven. D, a ram beside a river, was a still later vision of Daniel (see 8:2-4). And if you think I'm going to elaborate on choice E, YOU'RE the one who's dreaming!

7. A. See Daniel 12:9. The "abomination of desolation" (B) is discussed briefly in verse eleven. Choice C is found in 2 Peter 3:10, and D is located in 1 Thessalonians 4:16. As a Detroit Lions fan who's had so little to cheer about for so many years I've lost track, I wouldn't think it out of the realm of possibility that the end may come before a winning football team hits the Motor City.

III. For Spiritual Prophet

1. E. None of the above. It is found in Isaiah 1:18.

2. A. See Ezekiel 3:1-3. Keep this in mind, you never know when God may make you eat your words. P.S. If you have a prophet named Kevin

in your Bible, your Bible may have some collector value, but I wouldn't spend a lot of time reading "Kevin" for your spiritual benefit.

3. D. See Daniel 5:27. While this judgment was probably also appropriate for Judah (A), Babylon (B), and King Jehoiakim (C), it really wasn't Zacchaeus' fault if his weight was minimal. You see, he was a tax collector, which means he spent a lot of time running.

4. C. See Jeremiah 7:11. Actually in the first part of Matthew 21:13 Christ refers to the temple as a "house of prayer," which is a quote from Isaiah 56:7. But that wasn't the question, so don't be too quick to pat yourself on the back if you answered with choice B. It's wrong! If you answered E (Paul) that's only a minor mistake. You only missed it by one testament and roughly 650 years.

5. C. See Ezekiel 37:11. The valley of dry bones is a fascinating vision, so much so that it inspired the song. I guess you could say that God had a bone to pick with Israel. Or you could say that Israel needed to bone up on serving God. I'm glad YOU said that. (Hey— you can't expect me to hit your funny bone every time. Oops. . .another bonehead pun.)

6. B. Jeremiah 31:31-34.

7. D. See Isaiah 59:21. This was also a covenant guaranteeing God's word would be handed down. I really question God's need for a Triple A guide to Jerusalem. I mean, how many stars would a hotel have to have for GOD to stay there? On the other hand, Mary and Joseph couldn't even get reservations. But what if they'd gotten a room? Would we then, at Christmas time, instead of setting up the traditional manger scene, set up a double bed, some cheap furniture, a lamp, a clock radio, and a tub of ice with a Holiday Inn insignia on it, and call it a creche? Would the words to "Away in a Manger" be changed to, "Away in a Double with a Rollaway?" It's a good thing God worked out the details, right?!

TOTAL CORRECT ANSWERS:_____

SCORES. . .RIGHT THIS WAY

HOW DID YOU DO?

21–20: Excellent, if Isaiah so myself!!!

19–18: Like the handwriting on the wall, it's obvious you know your prophets!

17–14: Not bad, not bad at all. Not great, not great at all. (But not bad, not bad at all.)

13–9: This covers the fifty percent range, which considering the content and difficulty of the material is. . .STILL AN "E"! Ha ha ha.

8–4: If you REALLY, SERIOUSLY knew the answers to the questions that you answered correctly, few though they were, I'll let you off easily. But just this once!

3–0: I'll be expecting a fan letter from you! (Provided you can "guess" my address.)

CHAPTER FIVE AWAITS YOU. . .

On the other hand, doesn't a little nap sound better? I wrote most of the next chapter during mine. (You're not surprised, are you?)

THE MINER PROPHETS

SECTION FIVE

PROPHET
MINORS DOGMA

I. Prophet Potpourri

1. God instructed Hosea to:

   A. *Marry King Hezekiah's daughter*
   B. *Marry a harlot*
   C. *Remain unmarried*
   D. *Seek a virtuous wife*

2. Joel is initially concerned with:

   A. *An upcoming religious feast*
   B. *A war with Babylon*
   C. *A locust attack*
   D. *Idol worship*
   E. *Keeping his children occupied
      during summer vacation*

3. Amos prophesied approximately two years
   before what recorded disaster?

   A. *An earthquake*
   B. *A "great wind" (possibly a tornado)*
   C. *A flood*
   D. *A volcanic eruption*
   E. *Mandatory income tax withholding*

4. Which of the following are true concerning Obadiah?

   A. *His book is the shortest in the Old Testament*
   B. *There are thirteen Obadiahs in the Old Testament*
   C. *His book concerns the descendants of Esau*
   D. *His name was defeated by only two votes in favor of "Oklahoma" as the name of our forty-sixth state*

5. How did Jonah end up in the water prior to being swallowed by the "great fish"?

   A. *The boat he was riding in capsized*
   B. *He was swept off a ship by a large wave*
   C. *He jumped in to save another man*
   D. *He was thrown in by the sailors of the ship on which he was a passenger*
   E. *He was surfing in the Great Sea*

6. Micah offers a distinctly clear prophecy of which of the following?

    A. *The millennium*
    B. *The birthplace of Christ*
    C. *The battle of Armageddon*
    D. *The building of the new temple*
    E. *The fall of the Nixon administration*

7. Nahum may best be capsulized by which of the following?

    A. *Nahum's interpretation of a coming Messiah*
    B. *Nahum's prediction of an inevitable famine, and its outcome*
    C. *God's approaching judgment of Nineveh*
    D. *A warning to Jews concerning intermarriage with Gentiles*
    E. *Nahum's dissatisfaction with the fact that people could say his name while clearing their throat*

II. "Excess Prophets"
(Which means there's more than I know what to do with.)

1. God told Habakkuk that Judah would be over-
thrown by the Babylonians as a judgment
against them. Why was Habakkuk upset
about this?

   A. *Because he believed the Baby-
      lonians were even more wicked*
   B. *Because he believed he could con-
      vince Judah to repent*
   C. *Because he feared for the lives of
      his family and himself*
   D. *Because he despised war*
   E. *Because he realized the most probable
      route of Babylonian attack was across
      his favorite golf course*

2. Which of the following is NOT true concerning Zephaniah?

   A. *He was a descendant of King
      Hezekiah*

B. He prophesied judgment against the entire earth

C. He prophesied restoration for Israel

D. He prophesied the rise of the Roman Empire

E. He served as technical advisor for "The Ten Commandments"

3. Haggai is upset at his people because. . .

A. They are worshipping idols

B. They want to return to Babylon

C. They have ignored his call to repentance

D. They are not interested in rebuilding the temple

E. They have all "maxed out" their credit cards

4. Which of the following is NOT a vision of Zechariah?

A. A man with a measuring line

B. A woman inside a basket

C. A horse with golden wings

D. A flying scroll

E. A talking bagel

5. According to Zechariah, in the day that the Lord is King over all the earth, what inscription shall be engraved on the bells of horses?

    A. *Holiness unto the Lord*
    B. *Blessed be the most high God*
    C. *Worthy is the Lamb*
    D. *Do not forsake thy God*
    E. *Made in Taiwan*

6. Whom did God curse through Malachi, because they had not given Him glory?

    A. *"All inhabitants of earth"*
    B. *The priests*
    C. *The rulers of Judah*
    D. *The descendants of Esau*
    E. *The Democrats*

7. In the next-to-last verse of the Old Testament (see Malachi 4:5), who does God say He will send before the "dreadful day of the Lord"?

    A. *Michael the archangel*
    B. *Elijah the prophet*
    C. *"My messenger"*
    D. *The Comforter*
    E. *Gabriel*

And now it's time for. . .

III. Name That (Minor) Prophet

1. This minor prophet declared that he "was no prophet" nor "son of a prophet," but "a herdsman and tender of sycamore fruit." He was. . .

    A. *Jonah*
    B. *Micah*
    C. *Amos*
    D. *Joel*
    E. *Willing to work his way up*

2. His father's name was Cushi. His name was. . . (good luck)

    A. *Zephaniah*
    B. *Zechariah*
    C. *Malachi*
    D. *Nahum*
    E. *Lil' Cush*

3. This prophet had a wife named Gomer (not Pyle). He was. . .

    A. *Obadiah*
    B. *Joel*
    C. *Habakkuk*
    D. *Hosea*
    E. *None of the above*

4. This prophet was mentioned by Ezra as working with Zechariah in helping rebuild the temple. He was. . .

    A. *Malachi*
    B. *Joel*
    C. *Haggai*
    D. *Micah*
    E. *CEO for Temple Builders, Inc.*

5. This prophet was unhappy about a revival that he was instrumental in creating. Name him.

    A. *Zechariah*
    B. *Habakkuk*
    C. *Nahum*
    D. *Jonah*
    E. *None of the above*

6. This prophet had three children, named Jezreel, Loruhamah, and Loammi. He was. . .

    A. *Zephaniah*
    B. *Zechariah*
    C. *Joel*
    D. *Nahum*
    E. *None of the above*

7. This prophet was referred to by Christ as "murdered between the temple and the altar." He was. . .

    A. *Zacharias*
    B. *Haggai*
    C. *Micah*
    D. *Amos*
    E. *Having a bad day*

U.S.D.A.
OFFICIAL ANSWERS
(Unusually Silly Delirious Author)

I. Prophet Potpourri

1. B. See Hosea 1:2. God used Hosea's marriage as a comparison between Himself and His chosen people.

2. C. There had been an extremely serious attack of locusts (see Joel 1:4-7). While religious feasts (A), wars (B), and idol worship (D) were always a concern of prophets, nothing was quite so taxing as keeping the kids occupied in the summer (E). In fact, one of Joel's greatest prophecies is not recorded in the Bible. It was when he told his kids, "If you don't behave, you will know the wrath of God."

3. A. An earthquake. This probably took place

about 753 B.C. Concerning choice E, let me say that the real disaster is not in the withholding itself, but rather what they spend it on after they take it! Is there an "Amen" in the crowd?

4. A, B, and C are all true. I believe the main reason his name wasn't considered for the state is because Rogers and Hammerstein didn't like the sound of "you're doin' fine Obadiah. . .Obadiah ooookay!"

5. D. See Jonah 1:15. Interesting reading. You could say it's a whale of a story, but that's a really poor attempt at humor. You could say there's something fishy about it—that also being a sad effort. Therefore you may conclude concerning my witticisms, the same thought that was in the mind of the great fish as he began to feel Jonah sliding down his throat. "Some things," he thought, "are just a little hard to swallow."

6. B. Micah prophesied that the Messiah would be born in Bethlehem some 700 years before it took place. I wonder why he didn't make a reservation at the inn so that Jesus wouldn't have to have been born in the stable. Of course, he may have tried to, but was told

they didn't take reservations that far ahead. ("Um, sir. . .call us back in about 650 years, okay, sir? Sir? Sir?")

7. C. Nahum predicted the fall of Nineveh, one of the greatest cities of its time. While its people had repented as a result of Jonah's warning a century earlier, they had since returned to their sinful ways. About choice E: The reason you can say Nahum's name while clearing your throat is because that is actually how he got his name. You see, in the old days, women were unquestionably subservient to their husbands. When Nahum was born, his mother said to his father, "What shall we name our son?" Her husband was, at the time, suffering from a cold. Before he could speak, he cleared his throat. "Naaumm, naaumm," he said, to which his wife replied, "A little unusual, I guess, but then this IS the Old Testament."

II. "EXCESS PROPHETS"

1. A. See Habakkuk 1:12-17. Habakkuk was concerned about the wickedness of Babylon,

and questioned God's choice of that nation to be a part of Judah's judgment. While alternatives B, C, and D may be true, we have no basis for proof. We know very little about Habakkuk. His concern for his favorite golf course (E) was legitimate however. In fact, the Babylonians nearly retreated as they crossed the fairway on the third hole and saw Jerry Ford about to tee off.

(Not to hurt Habakkuk's feelings or anything, but the golf course was really not that great of a loss. The only carts they had available were pulled by oxen.)

2. D. Zephaniah does not mention the rise (or fall for that matter) of Rome. A, B, and C are all true. (No Scripture references given, just read the book. C'mon, it's only three chapters!) Zephaniah was not technical advisor for "The Ten Commandments," although Mr. DeMille wanted him. When Zephaniah found out that Charlton Heston beat him out for the part of Moses, he walked off the set.

3. D. Haggai, as one of the spiritual leaders of the Jews who had returned from Babylonian

exile to their homeland, wanted to see the temple rebuilt.

4. C. For the "genuine" visions, see Zechariah chapter two (A), chapter 5 (B and D). No mention is made of a horse with golden wings. Of course, the "talking bagel" is my attempt at humor. However, talking food does exist. There is the "snap, crackle, and pop" of that famous cereal, and talking margarine that says "butter," just to name a couple. I guess most talking food I've met is the kind that gets in your stomach and then starts screaming to get out.

5. A. See Zechariah 14:20. B through D are found in various other parts of the Bible, but I'm growing tired of researching all of the wrong answers. If you want to know where they are. . .FIND THEM YOUR-SELF!!

I'm sorry, I don't mean to shout like that. Uh, er, let me look up those other selections for you. Okay, letter B comes from Genesis 14:20. C, "Worthy is the Lamb," comes from Revelation 5:12. D, "Do not forsake thy God," is my own interpretation of Deuteronomy 32:15. Finally, you'll need to do a little research to find out where choice E is found. In fact, you'll have to look long and hard NOT to find it!

6. B. God cursed the priests in Malachi, chapter two, for their corruption.

7. B. See Malachi 4:5. "Behold I will send you Elijah the prophet. . ." You will recall Elijah from the previous chapter. God will recall him just before the final one.

III. NAME THAT (MINOR) PROPHET

1. C. See Amos 7:14. While choice E was "tongue-in-cheek" (I always thought that was the name of some Indian comedian) it is interesting to note that God chose prophets from all walks of life. There still may be hope for me, but don't bet your last mite. (You "mite" lose it! Ha Ha Ha). (Of course, it's only a "widow" bit of money! HA!)

2. A. See Zephaniah 1:1. Zechariah's father (B) was Iddo the prophet. Both Malachi and Nahum's fathers' names are unknown. (That's

a funny name!) E, Lil' Cush, was Zephaniah's nickname, although people seldom called him that after he began preaching judgment against Judah.

3. D. See Hosea 1:3. Gomer was the harlot that God used to compare with His people who had turned from His righteousness. None of the other prophets listed as choices have any information about their marital status offered in the Bible.

4. C. Haggai (see Ezra 5:1-2). Note: The CEO for Temple Builders, Inc. (E) was later jailed after he was convicted of giving kickbacks to the Babylonians, in return for their helping create business for his company.

5. D. Hopefully this one was a little easier. Jonah had a bit of an attitude problem that most of us can probably relate to. No, not with ourselves, but with other people that we know.

6. E. None of the above. The correct answer is Hosea. He and Gomer had three children, and each of their names were given to further illustrate God's judgment on the people. See Hosea 1:3-9.

7. A. See Matthew 23:35. Many of the prophets

suffered untimely and cruel deaths. I am not even close to being a prophet, but I might surmise a similar fate should anyone ever read this book. Oh, well, nothing to worry about there!

For my opinion of your scores on Chapter Five, please go to the following page. There will be several blank pages at the end of this book where you can write your opinion of me!

Hello. . .What's this? You're finished with the Old Testament? And my writing career, which never really began, is also nearly over! There's two good reasons to celebrate!

TOTAL CORRECT ANSWERS: _____

HOW 'BOUT DEM SCORES...

21: Get real! (Actually, if you're telling the truth you're ready for the "minor" leagues!)

18-20: This is no "minor" accomplishment. Nice job!

15-17: Very good! (Unless you're under twenty-one. This book should not be in the hands of "minors.")

11-14: Still a good score. You just need some "minor" brushing up.

8-10: This is under half. Not a disgrace, but definitely room for improvement. Think of it as a "minor" setback.

5-7: Poor. Better than nothing. Your scores are about as bad as "mine are."

0-4: I'll bet if you see the word "minor" one more time you're going to scream, right?

PLEASE TURN TO THE NEXT PAGE...

"Minor"
(Somehow, you just knew it, didn't you?)
And now...
(trumpet fanfare)

THE NEW TESTAMENT

If you're still with me, take heart—the tough part is over! Well, most of it anyway. My experience has been that most people are much more familiar and comfortable with the New Testament, but I trust your sojourn in the Old was worthwhile, and added some previously unknown (or forgotten) information to your memory banks.

Regardless of all this, your mission stands one half completed. While the New Testament comprises only about one third of the Bible, it still contains half the material in this book. Feel free to pray before you continue. Amen. Now go for it!

SECTION SIX

CHRIST AND BEYOND

1. "Oh, I can never think of his name!"

1. According to Matthew, chapter two, who told Joseph that Herod wanted to destroy "the young child" (Jesus)?

> A. Herod
> B. The wise men
> C. An angel of the Lord
> D. Mary
> E. He heard it on the eleven o'clock news

2. Which of the following was not an apostle?

> A. Andrew
> B. John, son of Zebedee
> C. Lebbaeus, surnamed Thaddaeus
> D. Luke
> E. All of the above were apostles

3. What baptism took place in the first chapter of Mark?

> A. John the Baptist was baptized by Jesus
> B. Jesus was baptized by John
>   the Baptist

C. Mark was baptized by Jesus
D. Jesus baptized a eunuch
E. None. Baptisms were canceled
due to the monsoon season

4. Who was the blind beggar that Jesus healed while leaving Jericho?

A. Jairus
B. Bartimaeus
C. Barabbas
D. Dalmanutha
E. None of the above

5. According to Luke, chapter one, who was struck mute until his son was born?

A. Phanuel
B. Joseph
C. Simeon
D. Zacharias
E. "Quiet Sam"

6. The Book of Acts was most likely written. . .

A. By Luke, to Theophilus
B. By Peter, to "all the brethren"

C. *By Paul, to the Roman Church*
D. *By John, to "preserve the knowledge of Christ"*
E. *By George, you may have gotten one right!*

7. Who was appointed by the apostles to fill the vacancy left by Judas Iscariot?

A. *Joseph, surnamed Justus*
B. *Alphaeus*
C. *Matthias*
D. *Ananias*
E. *Judas' twin sister Harriet*

II. "Awesome!" Miracles of Christ and the Disciples

1. According to Matthew, which of the following is Christ's first recorded specific miracle?

A. *Healing Peter's mother of a fever*
B. *Cleansing a leper*
C. *Healing the centurion's paralytic servant*

D. *Calming the winds and sea*
E. *Solving Peter's income tax lia-
    bility problem*

2. Why were the disciples afraid when they saw Jesus walking on the water, toward the boat in which they were riding?

   A. *They were afraid He would drown*
   B. *They thought He would be upset
       at them for leaving without Him*
   C. *They thought they would capsize
       before He reached them*
   D. *They thought He was a ghost*
   E. *Because their radar hadn't detected
       anything*

3. According to Mark, chapter five, what happened to the herd of swine after Jesus allowed unclean spirits to enter them?

   A. *They ran off the side of a cliff and
       fell to their deaths*
   B. *They attacked each other*
   C. *They ran down a hill into the sea
       and drowned*
   D. *They made loud sounds and fell dead*

E. They collectively let out a loud sow
   of relief
F. They "pigged out"
G. They were "boared" to tears
H. They "hammed it up"
I. They had "gilt" feelings
J. They went hog wild
K. I think it's time to hang up the
   "pen"

4. According to Luke, chapter eight, who was healed by touching the hem of Christ's garment?

   A. A woman who had a "flow of blood"
      for twelve years
   B. A man with a "legion" of demons
   C. A mute
   D. Lazarus
   E. A seamstress

5. Per John's Gospel, to whom did Christ first appear following His resurrection from the dead?

   A. Simon Peter
   B. The "other disciple"

C. *Mary, Jesus' mother*
D. *Mary Magdalene*
E. *A, B, and D simultaneously*

6. Which of the following did NOT occur on the Day of Pentecost?

   A. *A sound from heaven, like a rush of wind, filled the house*
   B. *Christ appeared in their midst*
   C. *"Tongues of fire" sat on each of them*
   D. *They spoke with other tongues (languages)*
   E. *Jerusalem initiated its long awaited recycling program*

7. According to Acts 5, how were the apostles released from prison, allowing them to return to preaching in the temple?

   A. *An earthquake shook the prison and the doors opened*
   B. *The High Priest granted them a pardon*
   C. *An angel of the Lord opened the doors*

D. *The guards were blinded, allowing the apostles to escape*

E. *They were released on their own recognizance*

III. WHERE WERE YOU?!

1. Where did Joseph, Mary, and baby Jesus flee to upon the advice of the angel in Joseph's dream?

    A. *Nazareth*
    B. *Galilee*
    C. *Egypt*
    D. *Tyre*
    E. *Las Vegas*

2. According to Matthew, where were Christ and His disciples when He told Peter that he would deny Him three times?

    A. *Gethsemane*
    B. *The Mount of Olives*
    C. *The High Priest's courtyard*
    D. *The upper room*
    E. *None of the above*

3. In Luke 4:1, to what location was Christ led by the Spirit, where He was then tempted by the devil?

   A. *Into the desert*
   B. *Into the wilderness*
   C. *Up to a high mountain*
   D. *Upon a pinnacle of the temple*
   E. *A rest stop off Interstate 80*

4. In what city did Christ spend a day at Zacchaeus' house?

   A. *Jerusalem*
   B. *Bethany*
   C. *Capernaum*
   D. *Jericho*
   E. *Washington, D.C.*

5. In what city was Simon, a sorcerer, converted under Philip's ministry?

   A. *Jerusalem*
   B. *Samaria*
   C. *Gaza*
   D. *Ethiopia*
   E. *Camelot*

6. Where was Saul when his sight was restored?

    A. *Lydda*
    B. *Joppa*
    C. *Jerusalem*
    D. *Damascus*
    E. *At an Oral Roberts crusade*

7. On what island did Paul find himself after the shipwreck discussed in Acts 27?

    A. *Sicily*
    B. *Crete*
    C. *Melita*
    D. *Cyprus*
    E. *Hawaii*

BEST
SELECTIONS

(SOUNDS LIKE AN AD FOR A USED CAR LOT, DOESN'T IT?)

I. "OH, I CAN NEVER THINK OF HIS NAME!"

1. C. According to Matthew 2:13, "the angel of the Lord appeared to Joseph in a dream." Herod (A) asked the wise men (B) to inform him as to Christ's whereabouts so that he also could worship Him. (Get real, Herod. The wise men didn't get that name by being stupid). However, the wise men returned home a different way (Matthew 2:12). Joseph never watched the eleven o'clock news (E), because Mary (D) wouldn't let him. She used to tell him he was just too hard to wake up in the morning if he wasn't in bed by ten-thirty.

2. See Matthew 10:2-4. D, Luke, was not an apostle, but rather a physician who traveled with Paul.

3. B. See Mark 1:9. Postponing baptisms due to monsoon season (E) never happened as far as we know. Nor did John the Baptist ever take a Sabbatical.

4. B. Jairus (A) was the father of the young girl whom Jesus raised from the dead in Mark 5:41-42. Barabbas (C) was the murderer released by Pilate in Mark 15:15. Dalmanutha (D) was the name of the region where Christ and His disciples went immediately after the miracle of the loaves and fishes, found in Mark 8:1-10. The correct choice would then be Bartimaeus (see Mark 10:46-52).

5. D. Zacharias's son was John the Baptist, just in case you'd forgotten. It's an interesting story that's told in the first chapter of Luke. Read it! Phanuel (A) is found in Luke 2:36 as the father of the prophetess Anna. Simeon (C) in Luke 2:25 delighted in seeing the Child Messiah. Joseph (B) is well known as Christ's "step-father" and Quiet Sam (E) just seemed like an appropriate nickname for a guy who had been struck silent. And while we're on the subject, wouldn't it be nice to have the ability to strike people silent? Who would you nail first? I think I would strike. . .oh well, it's fun to dream isn't it?

6. A. See Acts 1:1. Luke is generally accepted as the author of Acts, and the "former account" mentioned here is the book of Luke.

7. C. Matthias was appointed in Acts 1:26. Ananias (D) was the dishonest grantor found in Acts 5:1-11. You might say he made a "killer deal." (Sorry, that's an old real estate adage). I've yet to read that Judas had a twin sister named Harriet (E). If he did, would her name have been Harriet Iscariot? OH! Alphaeus (B) is mentioned in Acts 1:13 as the "other" James' father. Choice A, Joseph, surnamed Justus, was the other person nominated for Judas' vacated position, but he was defeated by the lot (Acts 1:26). Apparently it wasn't his lot to be a disciple. There is, however, a good story about him that you may not have heard. (I'm on pretty solid ground here). Legend has it that he once visited one of Jerusalem's slow-food restaurants (fast food hadn't been invented yet) and was having some difficulty in getting the waitress to notice his presence. He finally resorted to complaining to the establishment's owner, who went to the employee and asked, "Why haven't you taken care of this customer?" "I'm sorry," came the reply, "I thought Justus had been served."

II. "Awesome!" Miracles of Christ and the Disciples

1. B. All of these miracles are found in Matthew chapter eight, but the first is the cleansing of the leper in 8:2-4. Jesus did give us some insight on dealing with income tax liability (E). The answer lies somewhere between Matthew 22:21 and Matthew 6:34! Peter did have a unique tax problem, though. You see, he was a fisherman, which meant he had a large net income.

2. D. Both Matthew's (14:22-27) and Mark's (6:45-51) accounts indicate the disciples thought Jesus was a ghost. I guess that's understandable, since you seldom cross paths with people who walk on water. It is NOT uncommon, however, to discover folks who THINK they do!

3. C. See Mark 5:13. Options A, B, and D would all be legitimate conclusions if you were unfamiliar with the text, but they're incorrect. Choices E through K were the incoherent ramblings of a man who has absolutely no business trying to write at two o'clock in the morning (or any other time, for that matter).

(I may not be the wittiest guy you've ever read, but I'm honest!)

4. A. See Luke 8:43-48. The previous question dealt with the man with the "legion" of demons (B) although you may not have realized it. Selection C, a mute, is found in Luke 11:14. This led to Christ's adversaries suggesting that he cast out demons by Satan's power. Lazarus (D) was already dead when Christ healed him. Since it's pretty hard to "reach out and touch someone" after you've checked out, that pretty much eliminates Lazarus. A point to ponder about choice E: Didn't Christ say you reap what you sew? Ha ha! I'll bet you're in stitches! (Sorry, just thought I'd needle you a little.)

5. D. See John 20:11-16. According to John's account, Mary Magdalene came to the tomb first, then summoned Peter and "the other disciple" when she saw that the stone was rolled away from the tomb. Christ appeared to Mary shortly after these things happened.

6. A, C, and D all occurred on the Day of Pentecost. Acts 2:2, 3, and 4, respectively, document this. Selection B would probably best be remembered as John 20:19, when Christ appeared to his disciples after His resurrection.

7. If A sounds convincing, it's because Paul and Silas had that experience in Acts 16:25–26. B, D, and E were all fabricated, (are you surprised?) leaving C as the correct answer (see Acts 5:17-20).

III. WHERE WERE YOU?!

1. C. Matthew 2:13-15. In perusing your maps, you'll discover that Galilee (B) was a region lying north of Samaria. Tyre (D) and Nazareth (A) were both cities in the Galilean region. Joseph and Mary thought briefly about fleeing to Las Vegas (E), but after discussing the angel's instructions, decided not to gamble.

2. B. See Matthew 26:30-35. After this they went to "a place called Gethsemane" (A) (see verse 36). Later, Peter denied Christ in the High Priest's courtyard (C). The upper room (D) is found in Mark 14:15.

3. B, into the wilderness. The high mountain (C) and pinnacle of the temple (D) are found during the temptation in Luke 4:5 and 4:9 respectively.

4. D. Luke 19:1 begins the story with Jesus entering Jericho. Jerusalem (A) and Bethany (B) were both close by, just to the southwest. Capernaum was wayyy up north in Galilee. Don't be too depressed if you chose E, Washington, D. C. You see, Zacchaeus was a tax collector, and if you knew that, then D. C. was a fairly logical decision.

5. B. The account of the spread of the gospel after Saul's persecution began, commences in Acts, chapter eight. Phillip's ministry in Samaria is recounted in verses five through twenty-five. Gaza (C) is mentioned in verse twenty-six as the area to which an angel instructed Phillip to proceed. Ethiopia (D) is noted in the very next verse as the homeland of the eunuch. If you chose E, you obviously were thinking of Merlin, not Simon. By the way, isn't a camelot where you'd go to purchase a camel? "Buy a camel, sir? One hump or two?"

6. D. See Acts 9:10-19. Saul was blinded on the road to Damascus, and healed three days later after he arrived there. Lydda (A) was where Peter healed a paralytic in 9:32-35. Nearby at Joppa (B), Peter raised Dorcas from the dead (9:36-41). Saul had planned to go "Christian hunting" with the knowledge that any take

would be bound and brought back to Jerusalem (C). Paul never had the opportunity to attend an Oral Roberts crusade (E). However it should be noted that Saul (who later became Paul) became one of Christ's most "oral" followers.

7. C. According to the Book of Acts, Paul and some other prisoners were on a ship headed for Italy. They left Caesarea (Acts 25:4) and landed at Sidon the next day (27:3). They set sail again and passed "under the shelter of Cyprus" (D, see Acts 27:4), then close to Crete (B), according to Acts 27:13. Sicily (A) is an island just southwest of the southern tip of Italy, but is not mentioned in this text. While Paul had heard from some that the Lord was in Hawaii (E), he naturally (and correctly) assumed they meant Jack Lord.

We've passed this way before! Here we all are at the end of yet another section quiz, and the anticipation is welling up inside us! Wait. . . maybe it's just heartburn! Well, whatever, let's proceed with your sum evaluation.

TOTAL CORRECT ANSWERS: _____

TALLY WHOA!

IF YOU HAD. . .

21-18: This is an "A." I've so far resisted using such an archaic grading system, but now that we're in the New Testament it's time to go with something old. Go figure that out.

17-14: This is a "B." It means you could've done Better but you didn't do Bad.

13-11: "C." Average, mediocre, commonplace. Almost makes you wish you would've done worse, doesn't it?

10-9: "D." You're on the edge of a Scriptural Deficiency Precipice. One slip and it's "pagan city."

8-6: This is a grade below "D." You may choose your favorite letter anywhere between E and Z.

5-0: Let's start from the beginning. Tell me about

your childhood. Were you happy? How did your parents treat you? Do you feel a need to punish yourself? Why did you buy this book?

Prepare for Chapter Seven. Is seven your lucky number? Eight? Three? How about six hundred eighty nine? Four thousand two hundred twenty eight? Sorry, there's not a chapter by that number. Good thing!

CHAPTER SEVEN
Look, a Letter from Paul! (Part One)

I. Humble Paul

1. According to Romans one, to whom did Paul say he was a debtor?

   A. *Jews and Greeks*
   B. *Greeks and Barbarians*
   C. *Jews and Gentiles*
   D. *Romans and Samaritans*
   E. *First National Bank of Corinth*

2. What did Paul say in Romans eight is "enmity against God?"

   A. *The carnal mind*
   B. *The law of death*
   C. *Idolatry*
   D. *Failure to forgive*
   E. *Country and Western music*

3. What two things did Paul say he did NOT come to the Corinthians with, according to 1 Corinthians 2:1?

   A. *Pomp and pageantry*
   B. *Threats and harsh judgments*

C. *The old law and the*
   commandments
D. *Excellence of speech or wisdom*
E. *A Coke and a smile*

4. What did Paul say he would not do if it made a weaker brother stumble?

   A. *Prophesy in the temple*
   B. *Speak in tongues*
   C. *Drink new wine*
   D. *Eat meat*
   E. *Stick out his foot*

5. How did Paul hope to present the Corinthian church to Christ?

   A. *As a shining beacon of the faith*
   B. *As a chaste virgin*
   C. *As an eternal weight of glory*
   D. *As living by the power of God*
   E. *As having the best men's soft-*
      ball team in the Roman Empire

6. What did Paul say the Galatians would have done for him because they accepted him so well?

    A. *Provided all of his food and shelter*
    B. *Made him their High Priest*
    C. *Plucked out their eyes*
    D. *Believed anything that he taught*
    E. *Loaned him their best chariots*

7. What did Paul say to the Ephesians concerning his rank among Christians?

    A. *"I consider that I am not at all inferior to the most eminent apostles"*
    B. *"I have not attained perfection, but I press on. . ."*
    C. *"But God has appointed me a leader of the brethren"*
    D. *(I) "am less than the least of all saints"*
    E. *"I'm in charge here!"*

11. PAUL LOVED THE THRILL THAT HE'D FEEL WHEN HE GOT TOGETHER WITH. . . GOD'S WONDERFUL PEOPLE.

(WONDERFUL, AND NOT—SO—WONDERFUL PEOPLE FROM THE LETTERS OF PAUL.)

1. To what Old Testament leader did Paul refer in his Romans 4 discussion of works and righteousness?

   A. Moses
   B. Solomon
   C. Daniel
   D. Abraham
   E. Ronald Reagan

2. "Even for this same purpose have I raised thee up, that I might show my power in thee, and that my name might be declared throughout all the earth." According to Paul, to whom was this Scripture referring?

   A. Christ
   B. Noah
   C. Pharaoh

D. *Nebuchadnezzar*
E. *None of the above*

3. Paul spoke of divisions among the Corinthian Christians in 1 Corinthians, chapter one. Which of the following were NOT claims of the people?

    A. *"I am of Paul"*
    B. *"I am of Silas"*
    C. *"I am of Christ"*
    D. *"I am of Cephas"*
    E. *"I am a Baptist"*

4. In his second epistle to the Corinthians, whom did Paul exhort as "my partner and fellow worker concerning you?"

    A. *Timothy*
    B. *Titus*
    C. *Apollos*
    D. *Luke*
    E. *The Shulamite woman*
       (hey—now there's a name from the past)

5. In his letter to the Galatians, who did Paul say had extended the hand of fellowship to him at Jerusalem?

    A. *James, Cephas, and John*
    B. *Peter, James, and John*
    C. *John, Barnabas, and Titus*
    D. *John, Matthew, and Mark*
    E. *John, Paul, George, and Ringo*

6. What "beloved brother and faithful minister in the Lord" did Paul say he was sending to the Ephesians?

    A. *Barnabas*
    B. *Silas*
    C. *Epaphroditus*
    D. *Tychicus*
    E. *None of the above*

7. Who was Paul's symbol of bondage in Galatians 4:25?

    A. *Lot*
    B. *Esau*
    C. *Hagar*
    D. *Judas Iscariot*
    E. *Al Capone*

III. Is There a Doctrine in the House?
(Concepts, Comparisons, and Commentaries of Paul)

1. What did Paul tell the Romans that you do when you judge another?

    A. *Condemn yourself*
    B. *Blaspheme God*
    C. *Make the cross of no effect*
    D. *Cause a weaker brother to stumble*
    E. *Win valuable prizes*

2. Why did Paul say salvation came to the Gentiles?

    A. *Because the elect have cursed God*
    B. *That all people may know Christ*
    C. *Because the veil of the temple was torn in half*
    D. *To provoke Israel to jealousy*
    E. *Due to extensive efforts by the Gideons*

3. What did Paul tell the Corinthians was wiser than men?

    A. *The mind of God*
    B. *The Law*
    C. *That which comes from above*
    D. *The foolishness of God*
    E. *Dolphins*

4. What spiritual gift did Paul tell the Corinthians to especially desire?

    A. *Healing*
    B. *Teaching*
    C. *Prophecy*
    D. *Tongues*
    E. *Baking cookies*

5. Why did Paul say he was given "a thorn in the flesh"?

    A. *"To assure that men would worship God rather than me"*
    B. *"Lest I be exalted above measure"*
    C. *"That I might better understand infirmity"*
    D. *"To prove that Satan can be overcome"*
    E. *"Because I once forgot to wear my sandals"*

6. In Galatians 5:2, Paul instructed the Galatians that if they became circumcised. . .

    A. *They would fulfill the law of the Gentiles*
    B. *Christ would profit them nothing*
    C. *They would be found justified by God*
    D. *They would be an example to the churches in Macedonia*
    E. *They might want to cut down on fluids for awhile*

7. Which of the following are components of the "armor of God" as described in Ephesians 6:14-17?

    A. *The shield of faith*
    B. *Feet shod with humility*
    C. *The helmet of salvation*
    D. *The breastplate of righteousness*
    E. *Wells-Lamont gloves*

There are your twenty-one questions. Now let's see if I'm able to come up with twenty-one answers. Wish us both luck! (We'll need it!)

YE OLDE ANSWERS

I. HUMBLE PAUL

1. B. Surprised? Paul said in Romans 1:14 "I am a debtor both to Greeks, and to Barbarians; both to wise, and to unwise." Although Paul was indebted to First National Bank of Corinth (E), he managed to avoid repayment for quite some time. You see, he signed for the loan in the name of Saul.

2. A. While God definitely is against idolatry (C), and failure to forgive (D), the answer based on Romans 8:7 is A, the carnal mind. Choice B is just something that popped from my head to the paper (much like the rest of the material). Did I mention E? Waaill how 'bout thaat!

3. D. With the exception of E, Paul could have said any of these. But you, unfortunately, must select one as the correct answer, and you're only right if you chose D.

4. D. The text here discusses meat that had been offered to idols, and displays yet another facet of Christianity that Paul exemplified. I, too, have given up the practice suggested in E. Of course in my case, I usually have to get it out of my mouth first!

5. B. See 2 Corinthians 11:2. Paul mentioned choice C in 2 Corinthians 4:17, and D was used in 2 Corinthians 13:4. A could be considered a paraphrase of Matthew 5:16, but that book has nothing to do with questions (or answers) in this section. Now that I'm cogitating on E, let's think about a World Class All-Bible Softball team. Solomon would run the main office. He would provide wisdom, and also have on hand a large inventory of cheerleaders. Job, with his unlimited patience, would be the coach. Noah would make an excellent umpire, since he never let rain stop a project. As pitcher, how about David, with his ability to "sling 'em" in there. Put Judas in the lead-off batter slot, since if he could get on base, his ability to steal would come in handy. Samson, with his uncanny strength and tendency to swing things, could provide hitting at cleanup. (One hurdle he would have to overcome: keeping his eye on the ball after it had been gouged out). Designated hitter:

Joshua. He could put it over the wall. Short stop, of course, would be Zacchaeus.

6. C. Although Galatians 3:1 and 5:7 hint that the Galatians were susceptible to different doctrines (see D), in Galatians 4:15, Paul literally says "ye would have plucked out your own eyes and have given them to me." But then, they might have lost sight of Paul's message. Arrggh!

7. D. If A rings a bell, it may be because you read it in 2 Corinthians 11:5. But we're talking Ephesians here, remember? B is found in Philippians 3:12, and C sounds fairly convincing I think—but then I made it up! Alternative E is generally attributed to Alexander Haig (how soon we forget!) See Ephesians 3:8.

II. Paul loved the thrill that he'd feel when he got together with. . . God's wonderful people.

1. D. Abraham was the logical example for Paul's explanation of grace versus works. Although Ronald Reagan (E), is not exactly a spring

chicken, it's unfair to assume he was around during Abraham's time. (Abraham Lincoln, maybe, but NOT Abraham Abraham!)

2. C. In Romans 9:17, Paul asserts that this scripture was intended for Pharaoh. For further Biblical information read verses 14-23.

3. B. The contentions among the members of the early Corinthian church are reported in 1 Corinthians 1:11-12. Mentioned here are Paul (A), Apollos, Cephas (D), and Christ (C). No one happened to name Silas (B), which allows us to conclude that it is the correct answer. Of course, it doesn't say that anyone said "I am a Baptist" (E) either, and it's probably just as well. Sounds to me as if the Corinthians were already confused enough.

4. B. Titus. See 2 Corinthians 8:23. Apollos was mentioned in 1 Corinthians 1:12. (See previous answer, also see Acts 18:24-28). Timothy (A) came aboard in Acts 16:1-3 and was called faithful in Philippians 2:22. Two letters were addressed to him which, obviously, bear his name and will be covered in Section Eight. (Bet you can hardly wait—I know I can't!) Luke (D), and the Shulamite woman (E), have made earlier appearances, and I believe and hope that this is their final encore. (But you never know.)

5. A. James, Cephas, and John (see Galatians
   2:9). Peter (from B) was mentioned prior in
   1:18 and again in 2:11, 14. Barnabas and
   Titus (from C) were already with Paul,
   according to 2:1, and Paul makes no reference
   to Matthew and Mark (D) in his letter to the
   Galatians (see 1:18, 19). John, Paul, George,
   and Ringo never extended the hand of fellowship, but did instead sing, "I Wanna Hold
   Your Hand," which is not the same thing. If
   you chose this answer, you probably need
   "help." And I don't mean the album.

6. D. Tychicus (see Ephesians 6:21-22). He was
   another of Paul's traveling companions, and
   delivered Paul's letters to both the Ephesians
   and Colossians (see also Acts 20:4).

7. C. While A, B, D, and even E could be examples of bondage in their own way, the scripturally accurate selection is Hagar (see
   Galatians 4:25 per the question).

III. Is There a Doctrine in the House?

1. A. See Romans 2:1. Blaspheming God (B) is
   found in various parts of the Bible and in

varying circumstances. Ask Herod for his opinion (Acts 12:20-23). C, making the cross of no effect, corresponds to 1 Corinthians 1:17. Causing a weaker brother to stumble, or rather, avoiding it, is a constant challenge. So is remembering what you read twenty minutes ago in Part One, question four of this section. It covers D. Judging another will probably not allow you to win valuable prizes (E), but you might consider selling Burpee seeds. (Hey kids. . .remember those ads?)

2. D. Paul said in Romans 11:11, ". . .but rather through their fall salvation is come unto the Gentiles, for to provoke them to jealousy." Choice B is a paraphrase of Ephesians 3:19, C comes from Matthew 27:51, and A was a fabrication (again). While Paul never heard of the Gideons, they certainly have helped to spread the gospel and are a fine Christian organization. I did hear about a hotel that was so plush that they didn't have Gideon Bibles in the rooms. Instead, they had Billy Graham come in and read to you.

3. D. The scripture used here is found in 1 Corinthians 1:25.

4. C. For a better understanding of Paul's exhortation concerning spiritual gifts, please read

1 Corinthians 14:1-25. Baking cookies (E) is not a spiritual gift, but rather a talent or learned skill. Paul never discussed cookies in any of his epistles published in the New Testament, but legend has it that his angel food cake was out of this world.

5. B. See 2 Corinthians 12:7. No one is certain just what Paul's "thorn in the flesh" was. One theory states he had a disfigured face, while another speculates a speech impediment. Whatever it was, Paul wrote that it was "given lest I be exalted above measure." So nobody's perfect. I can relate, Paul. 2 Corinthians 12:9 discusses infirmity (C) and 12:7 indicates Satan's role (D). A also hints at Paul's logic, but is not the correct or "best" answer.

6. B. Christ would profit nothing. Paul stressed to the Galatians that if they chose to live under the law, they would be subject to it in its entirety. Consequently, C and D are out. I'm not aware of a "law of Gentiles," as the law was originally given to the Jewish people (see Deuteronomy 4). While I'm not a doctor, and I was just a baby when I experienced the procedure, E does seem like good advice. (But then, what do I know!)

7. Correct armor is. . .A (see Ephesians 6:16), C (Ephesians 6:17), and D (Ephesians 6:14). B is close. The Bible says, "having your feet shod with the preparation of the gospel of peace." Not quite close enough! Wells-Lamont gloves (E) are optional. While Paul didn't consider them vital to spiritual warfare, Paul Harvey says they rank high in his program.

THERE NOW,
THAT WASN'T SO GOOD, WAS IT!

HOW MANY RIGHT? _____

Ha ha ha!! You've got to be kidding! You're not? OOOHHH. Well, maybe you'll do better on Section Eight. (Who are we REALLY kidding here anyway?!)

HERE'S HOW YOU STACK UP...

21-18: It's apparent you've spent some time Roman through the New Testament. Keep up the good works. (But remember what Paul said about it.)

17-14: You may be missing a piece of armor, but you're still in fairly good shape for battle. I'll be right behind you!

13-10: We're approaching shaky ground here. Tread lightly!

9-6: This score casts a shadowy Paul—oops, I mean pall over your demonstration of knowledge in this area. Bone up!!

5-0: Sometimes a person needs to hit bottom before they realize that there is no hope for them unless they admit their problem, and begin to pull themselves up by their own bootstraps.

EIGHT AWAITS!

What do you mean you can't do it right now because you have to go watch a documentary on channel seven titled "The Migration of the Brazilian Katydid"?

CHAPTER EIGHT

LOOK—
A LETTER FROM PAUL!
(PART TWO)

I. PAUL, BEARER OF GOOD NEWS.
(ENCOURAGEMENTS TO THE BRETHREN, AND SISTERN)

1. How did Paul tell the Philippians that they could fulfill his joy?

> A. By being "like minded"
> B. By seeing to the needs of Epaphroditus
> C. By being anxious for nothing
> D. By having no confidence in the flesh
> E. By erecting a statue of him in Pigeon Square

2. Which of the following are things that Paul told the Philippians to "meditate on" in Philippians 4:8?

> A. Whatever things are true
> B. Whatever things are just
> C. Whatever things are heavenly
> D. Whatever things are lovely
> E. Whatever things are low in cholesterol

3. Paul told the Colossians to "put on charity," and called it. . .

    A. *The Balm of Gilead*
    B. *The gift of Christ*
    C. *The bond of perfectness*
    D. *The essence of the cross*
    E. *"Warmer than my sleeping bag"*

4. According to 1 Thessalonians 4:11, to what three things did Paul instruct the Christians at Thessalonica to aspire, so that they might lack nothing?

    A. *Pray without ceasing*
    B. *Esteem those above you in the faith*
    C. *Lead a quiet life*
    D. *Remain unmarried*
    E. *Work with your own hands*
    F. *Mind your own business*

5. Which of the following are part of Paul's list found in 1 Timothy, chapter three, concerning requirements for bishops?

    A. *One who rules his own house well*
    B. *Able to prophesy*

C. *Must have a good testimony*
D. *Must have only one wife*
E. *Must have a villa in Boca Raton*

6. "All scripture is given by inspiration of God, and is profitable for. . ." Which do not belong?

A. *Doctrine*
B. *Reproof*
C. *Instruction in righteousness*
D. *Understanding the fall of man*
E. *Hostile takeovers and leveraged buyouts*

7. What did Paul tell Titus that "those who have believed in God" should be careful to maintain?

A. *Good works*
B. *A good reputation*
C. *The walk of faith*
D. *The care of the widows*
E. *Filters, belts, and hoses*

II. Toward Whom Would Paul Lean?
(Pauline People)

1. According to chapter two of Paul's letter to the Philippians, what three people did Paul hope would visit them soon?

    A. *Euodia, Syntyche, and Clement*
    B. *Epaphroditus, Titus, and Clement*
    C. *Timothy, Epaphroditus, and Paul*
    D. *Timothy, Titus, and Bartholomew*
    E. *First John, Second John, and Third John*

2. The Colossian church was most likely started by. . .

    A. *Paul*
    B. *Timothy*
    C. *Tychicus*
    D. *Epaphras*
    E. *Goliath*

3. Who did Paul send to the Thessalonians according to 1 Thessalonians 3:2?

    A. *Silvanus*
    B. *Timothy*
    C. *Archippus*
    D. *Luke*
    E. *None of the above*

4. Whom did Paul tell Timothy he had "delivered to Satan" in 1 Timothy 1:20?

    A. *Hymenaeus and Alexander*
    B. *"Certain Greeks"*
    C. *Nero*
    D. *The household of Onesiphorus*
    E. *All of the above*

5. Who was the only person left with Paul during his final imprisonment, discussed in 2 Timothy 4:11?

    A. *Demas*
    B. *Luke*
    C. *Mark*
    D. *Tychicus*
    E. *A local blind man who had been arrested for being a "peeping Tom"*

6. Whom did Paul tell Titus to "send. . .on their journey with haste, that they may lack nothing?"

A. *Artemas and Tychicus*
B. *Zenas the lawyer and Apollos*
C. *Nicopolis and Timothy*
D. *Philemon and Onesimus*
E. *Captain Kirk and Spock*

7. Paul's letter to Philemon was concerning. . .

A. *His dissatisfaction with Philemon's ministry*
B. *The death of Luke*
C. *Paul's plans to visit Philemon*
D. *A slave named Onesimus*
E. *Ed McMahon's Publisher's Clearinghouse Sweepstakes*

III. RANCHO PAULOS
(AND OTHER PLACES OF INTEREST TO PAUL)

1. Where was Paul when the Philippian church sent him an offering, according to Philippians 4:16?

    A. *Thessalonica*
    B. *Colosse*
    C. *Corinth*
    D. *In Des Moines, setting up a "Farm-Aid" concert*

2. Paul mentions the church of the Colossian "sister city" four times in his epistle to the Colossians. It is:

    A. *Troas*
    B. *Ephesus*
    C. *Antioch*
    D. *Laodicea*
    E. *Anchorage*

3. Paul told the Thessalonian Christians that they had become an example to the believers in what two regions?

A. *Philippi and Berea*
B. *Corinth and Ephesus*
C. *Thrace and Illyricum*
D. *Macedonia and Achaia*
E. *The Deep South and the Old West*
F. *Tippecanoe and Tyler, too*

4. In what city did Paul urge Timothy to remain, according to 1 Timothy 1:3?

A. *Troas*
B. *Ephesus*
C. *Tarsus*
D. *Antioch*
E. *Auntie Em*

5. Paul's second epistle to Timothy explained that Paul had been abandoned by all of his friends from. . .

A. *Rome*
B. *Greece*

C. *Asia*
D. *Macedonia*
E. *College*

6. Where did Paul leave Titus to set things in order, according to Titus 1:5?

   A. *Crete*
   B. *Corinth*
   C. *Sicily*
   D. *Rome*
   E. *A Seven-Eleven store in Athens*

7. According to Philemon 1:12, where was Paul sending Onesimus?

   A. *To the church at Ephesus*
   B. *Back to Philemon*
   C. *To the Roman Council, to seek Paul's release from prison*
   D. *Spain*
   E. *On a slow boat to China*

ANTHERS—
SECTHION EIGHTH

I. PAUL, BEARER OF GOOD NEWTH

1. A. Paul told the Philippians to be "like-minded, having the same love. . ."
   Epaphroditus (B) is discussed in Philippians 2:25-30. C, being anxious for nothing, comes from Philippians 4:6. D is from Philippians 3:3. Pigeon Square still doesn't have a statue of the apostle (E), but Paul would be pleased to know that his hand prints are still holding up well in Grauminowitz's Jewish Theatre.

2. A, B, and D. Paul did not feel the need to mention things that are heavenly, or things low in cholesterol. And the reason is that he obviously knew the two could not coexist.

3. C. Balm of Gilead is mentioned in Jeremiah 8:22, and is not to be confused with Ben-Gay. It is also not to be confused with the bond of

perfection, which is found in Colossians 3:14, and also happens to be the right answer.

4. C, E, and F. Unless you're familiar with this passage, you're probably surprised. And all this time you thought Ann Landers had a patent on MYOB. A, pray without ceasing, comes from 1 Thessalonians 5:17, while B is found in 5:12–13. D is expounded upon in 1 Corinthians 7:25-33. The best part of all this new found knowledge is that you can tell people to mind their own business, and know that you're on solid ground scripturally! (Just be careful.)

5. A, C, and D. See 1 Timothy 3:4, 3:7, and 3:2 respectively. Paul was only hoping for a villa in Boca Raton (E) for bishop's conventions, but it was not a requirement.

6. This information is located in 2 Timothy 3:16. Included are A, B and C. Understanding the fall of man is not mentioned. Neither is E, LBOs and hostile takeovers. Back in Bible days, a hostile takeover didn't involve dozens of banks, corporate raiders and the S.E.C. Instead, it was more likely to consist of men on horses or in chariots, who bashed their enemies' brains out with a club, ran them

through with a sword, or pierced their flesh with a spear. In short, it was much more civilized.

7. A. Filters, belts and hoses probably didn't exist in Paul and Titus's day, and no historian has ever produced a letter from Paul to Mr. Goodwrench. (Lucky for us, huh!) The care of the widows (D) was alluded to in James 1:27. The walk of faith (C) is from 2 Corinthians 5:7, and a good reputation (B) is from 1 Timothy 3:7. The answer, then, is good works (see Titus 3:8).

II. Pauline People
(Seems like I dated her a couple of times.)

1. C. See Philippians 2:19, 24 and 25-30. Eudoia, Syntyche, and Clement are found in Philippians 4:2–3. First, second and third John never visited the Philippians. They were extremely busy practicing for the "all Roman" synchronized swimming team.

2. D. Epaphras (see Colossians 1:7). Paul (A) obviously was directly involved. Goliath (E)

was not part of the Colossian church. His was called the "colossal" church. It was a humungus place, one pew per customer. Goliath had a good reputation there for awhile, but one day he showed up stoned (see 1 Samuel 17:49). After that he just lost his head (1 Samuel 17:51).

3. B. Timothy. While Silvanus (A) and Luke (D) were traveling companions and close friends of Paul, Archippus (C) is not as familiar a name. He is found in Colossians 4:17, and has some type of ministry. . .probably nursery worker.

4. A. Paul was decidedly unhappy with Hymenaeus and Alexander. He later stated in 2 Timothy 4:14, "Alexander the coppersmith did me much evil: the LORD reward him according to his works." A pretty good indication that the apostle had nearly expended his supply of forgiveness toward these men. While he also would have been happy to deliver C, Nero (Roman Emperor, A.D. 54-68, persecutor of Christians, practicing lunatic), to Satan as well, the Household of Onesiphorus (D), on the other hand was supportive of Paul (see 2 Timothy 1:16-18, 4:19).

5. Luke, B. Demas (A) had forsaken Paul (see 2 Timothy 4:10). Paul instructed Timothy to bring Mark (C) with him and come to visit him in prison. Tychicus (D) Paul had previously sent to Ephesus (see 2 Timothy 4:12). Peeping Thomas (E) was a brother to doubting Thomas, whom you'll recall from John 20:24-29. Other family members were: Coughing Thomas, (a heavy smoker), Crawling Thomas, (a heavy drinker), and of course the family comedian, Danny Thomas.

6. B. Zenas the lawyer, and Apollos (see Titus 3:13). (Of course, at 150 bucks an hour, why would a lawyer lack anything anyway?) Choice A is from Titus 3:12. C is only half "whom," as Nicopolis was a city where Paul spent the winter (probably comparable to Miami Beach). D is from Philemon. Paul never got to see Captain Kirk or Spock (E) but probably would've appreciated the luxury of being "beamed up" from time to time. By the way, do you suppose Paul's "thorn in the flesh" could have been pointed ears?

7. D. Paul's letter to Philemon was concerning Onesimus, Philemon's slave who had escaped and was later converted. Paul was never big on sweepstakes (E) after he was

burned big-time on an embossed parchment deal. The Greek Island cruise he supposedly won for ordering tons of stationery (he used a lot of it) turned out to be along the Asian Coast to Italy on an Alexandrian ship. Paul never put the "yes" sticker on again (see Acts 27).

III. Rancho Paulos—Places of Interest
(To see how you "placed". . .read below.)

1. A. Thessalonica. Paul spoke highly of the Philippians' generosity and specifically "thanked them for their support." Paul was never involved with "Farm-Aid" concerts (E). He had enough problems just trying to plant churches.

2. D. Time to get out the maps again! Troas (A) was a ways northwest of Colosse. Ephesus (B) was roughly 100 miles west. Antioch (C) was close, but the correct answer is D, Laodicea. It is mentioned in Colossians 2:1 and 4:13, 15 and 16. I don't know why Paul never visited Anchorage. Juneau? (Never throw away an old joke!)

3. D. Since choices A and B were cities, not regions, eliminate them. Selection C was right off the map and not necessarily out of Scripture.

4. B. The Ephesian church was one of Paul's priorities for Timothy, and Paul urged him to remain there, to protect and encourage true Christian doctrine.

5. C. See 2 Timothy 1:15. When Paul returned to Rome from Spain during Nero's rule, Christianity had been declared an illegal religion. Most of Paul's friends failed to support him out of fear for their own safety. Paul's college friends (E) had become "guppies" (Greek Urban Professionals) and rarely concerned themselves with religion. They had forgotten their earlier days of fraternity camaraderie. (Their frats in Greece were named after English letters.)

6. A. The Island of Crete was assigned to Titus by Paul, and the short letter bearing his name is the aging apostle's instructions to his young assistant. Titus was not interested in working at the Seven Eleven in Athens (E). He'd had his fill of retail working near the Acropolis at his father's Marathon station.

7. B. Paul was sending Onesimus, a former runaway slave, back to Philemon, his owner. Although he had been a help to Paul, Paul knew this was the right thing to do. When Onesimus returned, Philemon sent him on a slow boat to China (E). (Just kidding, of course. I forgot this was supposed to be serious.)

TOTAL CORRECT ANSWERS: _____

TALLY
WHAT?

21–18: Great job, Alexander!

17–14: Good job, Johnny B!

13–11: Average, Joe

10–7: Sub-par, Jack!

6–0: Terrible, Ivan!

And so ends our apostle epistle episode. Prepare for the end. As my good buddy Frank says,

"THE BEST IS YET TO COME, AND BABE, WON'T IT BE FINE!"

Or was it Paul Bunyan who sang that song? To his blue ox? Yeah, that's right. Boy that guy had a lot of hits!

Nine is up, and if your blood pressure is too, take a break. You really do look pale.

SECTION
NINE

FROM HERE TO ETERNITY:
HEBREWS—REVELATION

I. WHO DRINKS THE COFFEE HEBREWS? PEOPLE OF THE LAST BOOKS.
(WE'RE ABOUT TO BREAK "FRESH GROUND.")

1. The author of Hebrews describes this Old Testament priest as a great man, in chapter seven.

   A. Aaron
   B. Ezekiel
   C. Melchizedek
   D. Caiaphas
   E. The Shulamite woman
      (I just can't get her outa
      my head!)

2. What two people did James give as examples of faith working together with works?

   A. Rahab the harlot and
      Abraham
   B. Joshua and Caleb
   C. Noah and David
   D. Isaac and Joshua
   E. Adam and Eve

3. Who did Peter use as an example of a submissive wife?

    A. *Leah*
    B. *Gomer*
    C. *Ruth*
    D. *Sarah*
    E. *Elizabeth Taylor*

4. In 2 Peter 2, this person is mentioned as representing those who have "forsaken the right way."

    A. *Pharaoh*
    B. *Lot*
    C. *Balaam*
    D. *Aaron*
    E. *None of the above*

5. What Old Testament character was "of the wicked one," according to 1 John 3:12?

    A. *Saul*
    B. *Cain*
    C. *Jezebel*
    D. *Nebuchadnezzar*
    E. *Both C and D are mentioned*
       in this text

6. Who did Jude say had prophesied about "these (evil) men?"

    A. *Enoch*
    B. *Elijah*
    C. *Zechariah*
    D. *Daniel*
    E. *Jean Dixon*

7. In Revelation 20:7-9, who deceives nations into surrounding the "camp of the saints"?

    A. *The beast from the sea*
    B. *The "Great Harlot"*
    C. *The dragon*
    D. *Satan*
    E. *A disenchanted New Orleans football fan*

II. "HOME, JAMES!"
(MORE PLACES OF INTEREST)

1. To where did the author of Hebrews tell the people that they have come?

    A. *Mount Zion*
    B. *The city of the Living God*

C. *The heavenly Jerusalem*
D. *To a fork in the road*
E. *A, B, and C are all correct*

2. According to 1 Peter 3:19, where were the spirits Christ preached to immediately following His death on the cross?

    A. *Hades*
    B. *Prison*
    C. *Heaven*
    D. *In the air*
    E. *In a Jack Daniels bottle*

3. Where did Peter say they were with Christ, when they heard "this voice which came from heaven"?

    A. *Near the Jordan*
    B. *In the upper room*
    C. *Gethsemane*
    D. *On the holy mountain*
    E. *On the back nine at Burning Bush Country Club*

4. What city (cities) does Jude refer to as being immoral?

    A. *Sodom and Gomorrah*
    B. *Chorazin and Bethsaida*
    C. *Tyre*
    D. *Capernaum*
    E. *Houston, TX*

Note: The last three questions are concerning areas discussed in the last book of the Bible. Therefore I refer to this part as the "Revelation Location Interrogation!" (YOU WILL TALK!!)

5. Where was John when he wrote Revelation?

    A. *In a Samarian prison*
    B. *The island of Malta*
    C. *Philippi*
    D. *The island of Patmos*
    E. *On a cruise in the South Pacific*

6. Where were the four angels released from after the sixth angel sounded his trumpet?

    A. *Armageddon*
    B. *The bottomless pit*

C. *The river Euphrates*
D. *The Great Temple*
E. *Folsom Prison*

7. What city is destroyed in Revelation, chapter eighteen?

   A. *Jerusalem*
   B. *The New Sodom*
   C. *Babylon*
   D. *Nineveh*
   E. *Terre Haute, Indiana*

III. Hey, Jude!
(DOCTRINE, THEOLOGY, BIOLOGY, UROLOGY, ETC.)

1. What does the author of Hebrews say is a potential reward for entertaining strangers?

   A. *They may be angels*
   B. *They may become close friends*
   C. *They may find salvation through us*
   D. *They may return the favor when we are in need*
   E. *They may be Hollywood talent scouts*

2. According to James 5:15, what will save the sick?

> A. *The power of God*
> B. *Righteousness*
> C. *The spirit of Christ*
> D. *The prayer of faith*
> E. *Penicillin*
> F. *Early diagnosis*

3. What three facets of outward adorning did Peter instruct women to avoid in 1 Peter 3:3?

> A. *Wearing gold*
> B. *Putting on fine apparel*
> C. *Wearing jeweled rings*
> D. *Painting the face*
> E. *Arranging the hair*
> F. *Wearing designer sunglasses*

4. What did Peter refer to his body as, in 2 Peter 1:13, 14?

> A. *This corruptible flesh*
> B. *A tabernacle*
> C. *This shell*
> D. *This mortal coil*
> E. *A Winnebago (Peter was having trouble dieting)*

5. The book of 1 John ends with the instruction, "Little children, keep yourselves from. . .?

    A. *Immorality*
    B. *The evil one*
    C. *Trusting in the world*
    D. *Idols*
    E. *Staying up too late*

6. What did Jude state that the argument between Michael the Archangel and the devil was concerning?

    A. *The Great Flood*
    B. *Cain*
    C. *The body of Moses*
    D. *The authority of God*
    E. *The MVP in the 1968 World Series*

7. According to the final chapter of Revelation, which of the following are true concerning the Holy City, or New Jerusalem?

    A. *A pure river flows from the throne*
    B. *The city walls are inlaid with diamonds*

C. God's name shall be on their
   foreheads
D. The sun shall shine constantly
E. There will be a tree of life
F. The gates will close after the
   saints have entered
G. Only Sandi Patti music will be
   played

HERE'S YOUR DECAFFEINATED ANSWERS!

(OR SOMETHING CLOSE TO IT!)

1. WHO DRINKS THE COFFEE HEBREWS? PEOPLE OF THE LAST BOOKS.

1. C. If you wonder how you could have gotten the answer, let's try the process of elimination here, okay? You can forget the Shulamite woman (although I obviously can't). Caiphas (D) was a priest, but the question said "Old Testament" and "Cai" as his friends called him, was a New Testament priest. Aaron (A) was mentioned in chapter five as "called by God." Ezekiel is not named at all in Hebrews (poor guy). Melchizedek thus wins by default. (Default of de author of de book.)

2. A, although Joshua, Caleb, Noah, David, and
   Isaac all had their triumphs in both faith
   and works (see James 2:21-25). Adam
   and Eve (E) started out okay, but then Eve
   turned "fruity," and even though Adam
   considered her the apple of his eye, he realized the core of their relationship with God
   was not faith supported by works. Adam
   was pleasantly surprised, however, when
   Eve promised to turn over a new leaf.

3. D. See 1 Peter 3:6. Leah (A) was a submissive wife, even though Jacob didn't love
   her as much as he loved Rachel, her sister
   (see Genesis 29:30). A, however, is incorrect.
   Gomer (B) was submissive to almost everyone. Also incorrect. Ruth (C) was an excellent example of a godly wife (see Ruth.
   Of course it's in Ruth, where did you think
   it would be? Proverbs? Nice try!), but
   unacceptable here. If Elizabeth Taylor (E)
   was not a submissive wife, it wasn't for lack
   of opportunities.

4. C. Balaam. Remember him? He's the one
   whose donkey was barely edged out for a
   T.V. sit-com by Mr. Ed.

5. B. Cain. While this is quite a cast of qualified

candidates, Cain takes the honors. I guess Adam and Eve weren't that good at raising Cain (except with God), although I understand his potato chips are still doing well.

6. A. Enoch

7. D. Yep, old Satan is once again the culprit.

II. "HOME, JAMES!"

1. E. Yes, E is the correct answer, as the author of Hebrews used A, B, and C in Hebrews 12:22. The fork in the road (D) is where you are right now. If you take the high road, you put this book away. Your other alternative is to continue to allow me to insult your intelligence. What's your choice? Really? Oh good! Let's continue.

2. B. This scripture tells us He (Christ) went and preached to the spirits in prison.

3. D. On the holy mountain (see 2 Peter 1:18). Peter never played Burning Bush, as it was a

W.A.S.P. outfit. There is a legend though about a golf game between Moses and Jesus. It seems Moses and Jesus were playing golf one day, and had completed the fourteenth hole when an older, distinguished looking gentleman who was playing alone, caught up with them. "Mind if I join you on the last four?" he asked. Moses and Jesus looked at each other. "Sure," they replied, "be glad to have you." Now the fifteenth hole was about 295 yards with a large water hazard right in front of the green. Moses teed up his ball and hit an excellent shot. Just as the ball reached the pond, the water parted, and Moses' ball rolled up on the green, about six feet from the cup. "Great shot, Moses," said Jesus. "Thanks, Lord," Moses replied. Jesus teed up His ball and also hit it nicely. Just as it approached the pond, two tiny feet popped out from the ball, and it walked across the water to the green, where it came to rest about three feet from the pin. "Very nice," said Moses. "Thanks," said Jesus. The older gentleman then stepped up to hit. His drive sliced badly and went rolling into the woods, where an opportunistic squirrel, thinking it to be a nut, picked it up in his mouth and began running across the fairway. An eagle, flying high above, spotted the squirrel and swooped low, snatching both the squirrel and ball, and began flying away. Just as they flew over the green, the ball fell from the squirrel's mouth and dropped perfectly into the hole. "I don't believe it!" exclaimed Moses, aghast. "I do," replied Jesus. Now smiling, He turned to the older gentleman and said, "Nice shot, Dad!"

4. A. Yes, Sodom and Gomorrah, those evil city standbys. If you guessed, this was a pretty fair stab. Chorazin and Bethsaida (B) were mentioned by Christ as evil in Matthew 11:21-22. In the same text, Tyre (C) is specified as a city that will receive more tolerance in judgment than those cities. In verse 23, Capernaum (D) is depicted by Christ as worse than Sodom. So we've come full circle and where do we end up? In Houston, of course!

5. D. Revelation 1:9 states that John was "in the isle that is called Patmos." The island was a place of exile for some Roman prisoners. Some accounts say that John survived being put in boiling oil by his captors prior to his exile. Regardless, he recorded his revelations probably about 95 A.D.

6. C. Revelation 9:14 is the reference for this
question. Armageddon (A) is a reasonable
assumption, and is found in Revelation 16:16
as the gathering place for the final battle of
the kings of the earth. The bottomless pit is
addressed (if a bottomless pit HAS an
address) in Revelation 9, as well as 11, 17,
and 20 as the residence of Abaddon (the
beast), and finally as a prison for the devil.
D, the Great Temple, is something I just
threw in there to try and trick you. Please be
advised that according to Revelation 21:22,
John saw no temple in the "New Jerusalem"
because, as John put it, "For the Lord God
Almighty and the Lamb are the temple of it."
Now there's something to look forward to!
Folsom Prison (E) is clearly an impossibility.
Why? Because those angels would have to
have been imprisoned there for hundreds,
even thousands of years. And everyone
knows that even MURDER won't get you
more than five years in this country!

7. Babylon, C.

III. Hey, Jude!

1. A. Hebrews 13:2 says, "Be not forgetful to entertain strangers: for thereby some have entertained angels unawares." Choices B, C, and D are also possibilities. E, of course, is reaching. (Unless it happened to be one of Charlie's angels.)

2. D. The prayer of faith. Not to be confused with E, penicillin, the so-called "miracle" drug. We're talking a different kind of miracle (semantics again).

3. A, B, and E. Okay gals, this is the chauvinist author speaking. I mean me! So lay off the labels, jewelry, and $75.00 hairdos. Just be yourself. Yes, your plain-old, cheap-slobby-clothes, unkempt-hair, self. Now, isn't that better?

4. B. Peter referred to the body as a tabernacle in this text, as did Paul in 2 Corinthians 5:1. You may recognize D as part of the soliloquy William Shakespeare wrote for Hamlet, and E as the way you feel after you've eaten an excessively larger meal than you should have.

5. D, idols.

6. C. According to Jude, verse nine (don't ask what chapter. If you don't know which chapter of Jude I'm referring to, look up Jude in your Bible and take a guess), the argument was about the body of Moses. The reason they also argued about the MVP of the '68 Series is not in regard to who it was, but instead it was about what the letters stand for. Satan thought it stood for Most Vile Person.

7. A is true (see Revelation 22:1). B is false, although Revelation 21:19-21 tells of jewel-studded walls, 21 is not the final chapter, and no mention is made of diamonds. C is true (see Revelation 22:4). D is false. Revelation 22:5 says there will be no need of sunlight, due to light from God. E is true (see Revelation 22:2). F is false. (see Revelation 21:25). The gates are open all day, and there's no night! G is also false thank goodness, and the proof is in Revelation 21:4. (Just kidding Sandi! I like your music, but hey, eternity is a long time!)

TOTAL CORRECT ANSWERS: _____

NINTH INNING SCORES

21-18: Home Run! Take a bow!

17-14: Triple! (But slide into third!)

13-11: You're on. . .but only by error!

10-8: Strike two. . .

7-5: Pray for rain!

4-0: The minors don't want you either. (But maybe Steinbrenner is looking for a coach!)

APPENDIX

(This one definitely needs
to be removed!)

ARE YOU SURE?

1. The shortest person in the Bible was Zacchaeus.

    A. *True*
    B. *False*

2. The Bible tells us how to respond to those who sneeze.

    A. *True*
    B. *False*
    C. *No, but the Dead Sea Scrolls do*

3. What was James and John's last name?

    A. *Smith*
    B. *They had no last name*
    C. *Disciple*
    D. *Do—Dah*
    E. *Doe*

4. The apostles all shared one automobile.

    A. *True*
    B. *False*

5. Isaiah predicted that Jerusalem would have leadership consisting of extremely attractive women.

    A. *False*
    B. *True*
    C. *Not sure*
    D. *Don't care*
    E. *Asleep*

6. The first securities dealer is found in Genesis.

    A. *True*
    B. *True*
    C. *False*
    D. *False*
    E. *A and B*
    F. *A and C*
    G. *All of the above*

7. The Bible tells us to throw away our money.

    A. *Yes, it does*
    B. *No, it doesn't*
    C. *Maybe it does, but I'M not*
       going to!

8. The Pharisees were cigarette smokers.

    A. *This is a true statement*
    B. *This is a false statement*
    C. *The Surgeon General is convinced*
       that this book is harmful to your
       mental health

9. Judas Iscariot played an electric guitar.

    A. *True*
    B. *False*
    C. *No, but he was unreal on*
       synthesizer

10. Paul sometimes drove a sports car.

    A. *True*
    B. *False*
    C. *Is this book about finished?*

11. Other than the "great fish" which swallowed Jonah, no other type of sea creature is mentioned in the Bible.

    C. False
    B. True
    A. Why is this upside down?

12. To which of the following did Paul give instruction concerning their dog?

    A. Titus
    B. Timothy
    C. Philemon
    D. Luke

13. Does the Bible address the sins of Hollywood?

    A. Yes, I think it does
    B. No, I don't think so
    C. Well if it doesn't, it should!
    D. Why should it? Hollywood is a
       pure city!

14. Jesus addressed the result of a man moving from Ann Arbor, Michigan, to Columbus, Ohio.

    A. *True*
    B. *True*
    C. *True*
    D. *Do I get a choice?*

15. Paul was a very good actor.

    A. *True*
    B. *False*
    C. *No one knows, as Paul was never screen-tested*

16. Isaac gave Esau specific instruction about preparing eggs for Jacob.

    A. *True*
    B. *False*
    C. *No, but he gave Esau his pancake recipe*

17. The children of Israel spent some time with a local drunk.

    A. *True*
    B. *False*
    C. *Hic!*
    D. *Iz zis za last quezzion?*

Well, dear reader, this is it—our journey is almost over. I'm sure you're having very mixed emotions right now. (The definition of mixed emotions is watching your mother-in-law drive your new car over a cliff). The final set of answers is just around the bend. . .

So Buckle Up Your Bible Belt and Hang On!

ROOTS. . .
THE FINAL CHAPTER
I MEAN, OOOPS,
THE FINAL CHAPTER

ANSWERS

1. False. There were actually people shorter than Zacchaeus. They are (in "descending" order): Nehemiah (knee-high-miah), Bildad the Shuhite, (shoe-height), and finally, the Philippian jailer, who fell asleep on his watch. (You have to be extremely small to sleep on your watch.)

2. A, true. Matthew 5:44 says, "Bless those who kershew."

3. D. Matthew 4:21 states that James and John were the sons of Zebedee. He is mentioned in the song which utilizes his last name, "Zebedee Doo-Dah, Zebedee A!"

4. True. According to Acts 1:14, "They all continued with one accord."

5. B, true. Isaiah 3:4, "Babes shall rule over them."

6. A, B, and E (True). Genesis 21:10 mentions a bondwoman. She also handled CDs, stocks, and surrogate services.

7. True. "Cast your bread upon the waters" (Ecclesiastes 11:1).

8. True. See Matthew 23:24.

9. False! I mean come on! That's the most ridiculous thing I've ever heard of! (Although I guess he could have borrowed the "axe" of the apostles.)

10. A, true. See 1 Corinthians 4:21, "Shall I come unto you with a rod?" Paul was into what most of us would consider "old cars." (Anything made before Christ. Back then G.M. stood for Gentile Motors.)

11. C, false. See Song of Solomon 8:6.

12. B. Timothy had been trying to get his dog, Spot, to "fight the good fight of faith." Paul

realized that while this was commendable, it was fruitless. He therefore instructed Timothy in 1 Timothy 6:14 to. . ."keep this commandment without spot."

13. A. Job 25:5 says, ". . .the stars are not pure in his sight."

14. A, B, C. TRUE!! See Matthew 12:45. ". . . and the last state of that man is worse than the first."

15. B. You'll want to read this for yourself. See Acts 19:31.

16. A, true. (Looks like a pattern forming here. Nope, just a little mold from the author's brain!) Oh, by the way, the reference is Genesis 27:40.

17. A. True again! Numbers 33:13, 14 discuss the children of Israel and a lush. There apparently was no water to drink there, so everyone just consumed spirits. And then they wondered why everybody was a lush! They were so inebriated they wandered around for FORTY YEARS!

GRIDIRON
BOX SCORE

(I HAVE NO IDEA WHAT THAT MEANS, BUT IT SURE SOUNDS IMPRESSIVE!)

17–15: Touchdown! Spike the football, your hair, or your dog!

14–12: Field Goal! The crowd goes wild! Hold out for a better contract!!

11–9: First Down! Nice play, but you still have forty yards to go!

8–6: Third and nine. This better be good!

5–3: Fourth and eight. Poor execution.

2–0: Punt. It's gonna be a long season.

RAP UP

Thanks so much for journeying through the Bible with me! I hope you've enjoyed the trip, and I'll see you along the trail, as soon as I've finished. . .

A. *Vacationing in Rio on the profits*
B. *Lecturing some theologians at Moody Bible*
C. *Signing autographs in New York*
D. *Meeting the President in D.C.*
E. *Filling in for the Pope*
F. *Waking up from a terrible nightmare about a book burning*

GOD STILL HAS THE ANSWERS!

BRAD

ACKNOWLEDGMENTS

SOME VERY SPECIAL PEOPLE...

My father, Carl Duane Densmore, to whom I'd like this book to serve as a living memorial. Although he succumbed to pancreatic cancer in 1993 at a "very young" sixty-five years old, just prior to his diagnosis eight months earlier, he was still flying kites and roller skating. He was happiest when he could make others laugh, and taught us all not to take ourselves too seriously. Thanks, Dad!

My mother, who is still very much alive and well, and has always lived for her family. Like most good moms, her biggest fault is that she worries too much, but makes up for it with outstanding meals, cookies, pies, and hugs. If I have any redeeming qualities, I owe most of them to this special lady.

My wife and best friend, Cathy. Thanks for putting up with my warped sense of humor all these years, and for keeping me somewhere near the borders of good taste (hopefully close enough!) with this book!

My daughter, Sarena Hammel, who also endured much of the "test material" that eventually became this effort. Unfortunately, Sarena has developed a sense of humor that resembles her father's (always loved that kid!). Although you have a different last name now, you will always be my daughter, and that makes me happy.

And last, but certainly not least, I'd like to thank my good friend Jim McClellan. Jim's early comments and encouragement regarding the manuscript were invaluable and his persistence that it should be published was greatly instrumental in my pulling it from the shelf and submitting it for the publisher's scrutiny.

And ultimately, to God, who has given us all things to enjoy. . .including laughter, one of God's greatest gifts.